# John McDermott

# John McDermott

## IT'S NOT ALL BLACK & WHITE

## John McDermott & Simon Ashberry

I would like to dedicate this book to my sister Ann, who died of breast cancer when she was 40.

I have such admiration for her. People often wrongly talk about bravery in football – she really was the bravest person I have ever known. Ann was always proud of what I had achieved in football and, despite what she was going through, she came to both Wembley games because she wanted to be there for me.

When she was undergoing treatment for her illness, Ann suffered hair loss and had blisters on her hands so her skin became red raw but you would never hear her complain – she was always laughing despite everything.

John McDermott

First published 2013

The History Press
The Mill, Brimscombe Port
Stroud, Gloucestershire, GL5 2QG
www.thehistorypress.co.uk

© John McDermott & Simon Ashberry, 2013

The right of John McDermott & Simon Ashberry to be identified as the Authors of this work has been asserted in accordance with the Copyrights, Designs and Patents Act 1988.

British Library Cataloguing in Publication Data.
A catalogue record for this book is available from the British Library.

ISBN 978 0 7524 9264 3
Typesetting and origination by The History Press
Printed in Great Britain

# Contents

# Acknowledgements

I would like to thank the following people:

My wife Dawn and her family Allan, Ann, Ashley and Lesley; my kids Ryan, Lauren, Charlie and Harry; my mam and dad, sisters Michelle and Marie and their families for backing me from day one. Not bad for a lad from Joe Wallies, eh?

John, Nicky, Scott and Craig Fraser for looking after me so well in those early years – not only me but my whole family. You are my second family. John, I owe you everything so thank you mate. Good memories.

Marcus Newell, his brother Dave, mum Veronica, dad Dave and sister Dawn – without you I would have gone back to Boro in the first year I was here. Marcus, not only my best man but a true friend.

Lee Stephens for looking after me from 16 to now. You gave me a start after football. You are a legend mate, I know you will always be there for me.

Dave Moore, my youth coach. Thanks Dave just for being you. Without you all this wouldn't have happened. A true Mariner. His brother Kev died aged just 55 while I was writing this book. Kev was a true pro and a role model for all us YTS lads. He looked after us and was a hero to us all. A true Grimsby legend, it was an honour to play in the team as him.

Simon Ashberry – thanks Simon for all the tireless work you have done, all the hours you have put in, the running around chasing people up. I am very grateful to you and really enjoyed working with you. My round next! Also a big thank you to your family as I know what it's like when you're not around spending family time. Cheers mate.

And most of all the people of Grimsby, not just the fans but the whole of the Grimsby public. You have always supported me from when I was young to now. You have given me and my family a great life and great memories for which I will always be in your debt. I am not just an ex-player but a fan of Grimsby for life. I cannot put it into words how grateful I am. I hope you enjoy the book and thank you all once again. UTM (Up The Mariners!).

Macca

The authors would like to thank the Grimsby Telegraph, the Press Association and the Professional Footballers' Association for kindly giving permission for several photographs to be reproduced in this book.

# Foreword

When I first joined Grimsby Town in 1988 there were only about seven experienced players registered and one or two youngsters, one of whom was a 19-year-old John McDermott.

I was told he could play two or three positions. He had been tried on the left wing and even as a centre-forward.

I looked at his main attributes, which were his pace and athleticism, and thought I would play him at right-back. And the biggest accolade I can give to Macca as a player is that through all the many years that I was at the club, I replaced strikers, midfield players, centre-halves, goal-keepers and wingers but I never ever had to look for another right-back.

Nobody ever used to beat Macca for pace. People used to play on his size on the back post but he was so athletic and had a really good spring that he was very rarely beaten in the air. His recovery was first class because of his pace and as the club progressed, his link-up play with wide-men and front players improved beyond all recognition. He was such a good all-round full-back, both defensively but also join-ing in attacks. You would have to go a long way to find one better in Grimsby Town's history.

He was also a model of consistency. Whenever he was fit, he played. You never had to think about dropping Macca because he never had a bad game.

Of all the successes that we had together, one of the most memorable was when I came back for my second spell and we went to Wembley twice. It was the first time in the club's history that Grimsby had been to Wembley and it was fitting that in the Auto Windscreens Shield final he won the man of the match award. I even remember him having a couple of shots that day, which was unlike him!

To have played so many games for a single club is a great achievement, almost a one-off these days. The thing about Macca was that from an early age he was clearly going to develop into a player who would be far, far better than the standard of the old Fourth Division. Luckily for the club we were promoted twice within two or three years. If we had been stuck in the Fourth Division Macca's ability would have been too good to stay there and I think he would have moved on. But as we moved up the divisions and found ourselves playing at a really good level against good teams, he was happy with that and felt he was playing at the level he deserved to be at.

During my time at Grimsby, the club was a fantastic place to be, particularly the first two spells. The dressing room was brilliant. Macca always seemed to be at the periphery of all the fooling around that used to go on although I think he was actually more involved in it than he used to let on. He was such a good lad, so polite and unspoilt, he never seemed to be any trouble at all.

He was a big mate of Mark Lever, they were always palling about together even though they looked like *The Odd Couple* because Mark was 6ft 3in and Macca was 5ft 7in. They went through the age groups as friends from the youths and reserves into the first team and played together for many years.

Macca was really keen on the coaching aspect of things, particularly in my last spell, as his playing career was coming to an end. He used to like to have a chat with me about things in training so he could learn the ropes. After over 700 games he has got so much to offer and it is good that he has found a niche to put that experience to good use. Eventually he'll want to go on to bigger and better things should the opportunity arise.

He made me feel very proud when he won the PFA Merit Award. I must have been one of the first people he rang to ask to go down to the ceremony and be one of his guests. When he received the award and Jeff Stelling asked him who had been the biggest influence on his career, he just looked at me and said, 'Well, he's sitting down there.'

I do still keep in touch with Macca a lot and I know he would dearly like the opportunity to manage Grimsby Town one day. Quite a few things have got to fall into place for it to happen but I would love to see Macca given the chance to have a crack at it.

Alan Buckley
Grimsby Town manager 1988–94,
1997–2000 and 2006–08

The Professional Footballers' Association Merit Award is the true Football Hall of Fame and the recipient is chosen by all the players on the Management Committee of the PFA.

The PFA Awards have been in existence since 1974 and recipients have included worldwide icons such as Pele and Eusebio and great managers such as Sir Alex Ferguson, Bill Shankly, Bob Paisley and Bill Nicholson; great players from these islands such as Sir Tom Finney, Sir Bobby Charlton; and great players who have become great managers such as Sir Bobby Robson, but the PFA has always been very keen to acknowledge those heroes who provide the backbone of the game and who have given magnificent service to their clubs often from outside of the top division and in so doing have shown not only supreme dedication, fitness, longevity and skill but also great loyalty to their clubs and above all to their profession.

Such recipients have included John Trollope, Tony Ford and Graham Alexander and in 2009 the Management Committee were delighted for the award to be presented to John McDermott who spent his entire twenty-year playing career at Grimsby Town FC from 1987 to 2007, covering three decades and holding the club's all-time appearance record, and becoming one of only seventeen players in the history of English football to play more than 600 Football League matches for a single club.

Throughout his twenty-year career John experienced promotion or relegation nine times, had two testimonials and was considered one of the top fifty players outside of the Premier League. He also won the man of the match award in Grimsby Town's Auto Windscreens Shield victory in 1998.

The very high regard in which he is held by fellow professionals and the football public showed itself in his final Football League game for Grimsby Town away to Shrewsbury Town when John was substituted in the 73rd minute and upon him leaving the field, play stopped briefly with both sets of fans applauding him off the field.

His place with the good and the great of football in the PFA's Hall of Fame is thoroughly deserved and he really is a 'true local hero'. It is a real privilege to be able to speak about someone who has given so much to the game they love and I am equally sure that all readers of this book who are genuine football lovers will more than appreciate a real player and a true role model.

Gordon Taylor OBE
Chief Executive
Professional Footballers' Association

John was one of the senior players when I went to Grimsby in 2000 – in fact he had already been playing for the first team for something like thirteen years.

Goodness knows how many managers he must have played under by the time he retired. But he was still going strong when I arrived and carried on playing for several more seasons after I left. Not many players get to have two testimonials at the same club – that's a real tribute to him.

In my time at the club, he was always a good pro who never let you down. You never had to consider playing anybody else at right-back, it was his position. John knew the game and he knew the position inside out.

He was enthusiastic, had a good sense of humour and was never any trouble. He just got on with it. In fact, John was exactly the sort of player any manager would want in their team, especially if it came down to a battle, he was just what the doctor ordered.

At his best John was a good Championship right-back and at his peak he would have counted himself a little bit unfortunate not to have played in the top flight.

One of the impressive things about John was that even after all those years playing he was still very receptive to new ideas. I brought in a lot of sports science to the club. It was when sports science was just starting to get cracking and he took it all on board even though he had been around for so long.

I had a great year at Grimsby, we stayed in the First Division (as it was then) and John was a big part of that. It was a terrific effort by all concerned to keep a club like Grimsby in that league against the odds. I brought in four or five foreign players but I also relied heavily on a small nucleus of really dependable players, of whom John was one.

I always thought he might become a manager one day because he knew the game, he knew what he wanted and he was well respected. I helped him get started with his coaching and it is good to see he has found himself a niche in the game after retiring from playing.

Mind you, he must have been disappointed that he wasn't given a go on the staff at Grimsby in some capacity.

When I was his manager, I knew John would go on playing as long as he possibly could and winning the PFA Merit Award in recognition for the length of his career at Grimsby was a very worthy honour for him.

John was always a big favourite with the fans because of his consistency and loyalty to the club. During my time at Grimsby we had a great League Cup win when we beat Liverpool at Anfield. John couldn't play that night because he was injured but he went to the game and sat in the crowd with the Grimsby fans. That sums him up more than anything else.

Lennie Lawrence
Grimsby Town manager, 2000–01

# 1

# The Longest Arms In Town

Grimsby has been my home for more than half my life now but my story starts in Middlesbrough. That is where I was born and bred, in a town that has always been a hotbed for football.

In recent years there have been internationals like Jonathan Woodgate and Stewart Downing but there has also been a long line of players from the town going right back to Wilf Mannion, who was a Boro legend either side of the Second World War. He was known as the Golden Boy because of his blond hair and there is a statue of him at Middlesbrough's ground.

In between, Middlesbrough has also produced the likes of Brian Clough, Don Revie, Chris Kamara and Peter Beagrie.

When you are brought up with that sort of history, it's easy to get caught up in the excitement of playing football from a very early age – and that's certainly what happened with me.

I went to a junior school in Middlesbrough called St Pius where the school team had a really good reputation.

The school team was only really for fourth years as we called them in those days, the oldest lads at St Pius before they moved up to senior school. You pretty much had to be in that top year to have a chance of playing in the school team and as we didn't have any other teams for the younger kids that was your only chance of playing in a proper match.

When I was younger I started to go and watch them play and I was determined to be out on that pitch. I would think to myself, 'I'm good at footie. I want to be in that team.' At that stage, they were still three years older than me and I was only small so there was no chance.

But the next year, when I was still two years younger than all these bigger lads, I managed to force my way into the team. It was unheard of. You never normally got in to the school team when you were only a second year, no way.

I remember getting the kit – even that was really exciting although it was massive and didn't fit me properly! The other lads playing seemed massive too but it didn't bother me.

The day before the first game I was so excited I couldn't really think about anything else all day and I ended up wearing my football kit to bed. I was really worried that I might lose it or forget to put it in my bag so I thought the best thing to do was just not to take it off at all. So I had my boots on and everything in bed – my mam wasn't very happy about that but it was the best way of not forgetting anything as far as I was concerned.

We used to go straight to matches after lessons so you had to bring your kit and your boots and shin pads with you into school. But on one occasion I forgot my pads. There was no way I was going to have time to get back home after school to fetch them so I nicked out of class.

Now this was a junior school, remember – kids are always doing that sort of thing in seniors but that's not what generally goes on in junior school. Certainly not back in the 1970s. I knew that my house was only ten minutes away and thought no one would miss me so I bombed there and bombed back.

But the teacher who ran the football team found out that I had missed lessons and asked me where I had been. I told him straight, 'I had to go home and get my pads for tonight, sir.' I thought he would be pleased that I was so keen to play.

But he was furious. Instead, he decided that I needed to be taught a lesson for skipping school so he just dropped me from the team there and then and told me I wasn't playing.

I was absolutely mortified. And ever since that day I hate being late for anything, for any meeting, any game. In fact, I'll often get there half an hour early – and it all goes back to that day at junior school.

What made it even worse on that occasion when I bunked off to fetch my shin pads was that my mate got picked to play instead of me. I was so gutted I spent the whole game wishing he had a stinker so I could get back into the team the following week.

Eventually I did start playing for the school team again and the following year we won a five-a-side tournament. It was the first trophy I had ever won and it meant a lot to me even though it was only a tiny little thing, six inches high.

We had some really good players in that side. There was a lad called Michael Shildrick, who was our Dennis Bergkamp – he should have really made it as a footballer but didn't. And we had a lad in goal called Patrick McElwee who was a bit like the Sylvester Stallone character in *Escape to Victory*. He had never really been in goal before but ended up playing there for us and he was brilliant – he was like a cat! He was as hard as nails and used to threaten anyone who came near him, a great character to have in the team.

When it came to having the team picture taken with the trophy, the photographer said to me, 'Lean in, son, you don't want to miss out being on the picture.' But I must have got flustered and ended up leaning the wrong way! When you look at that photo now, I look a mess. Everyone is normal apart from me – I'm leaning so far over it looks like I have had a stroke and am about to collapse.

It was the first team photo I had ever been part of but our strip was like Sunderland's, red and white stripes. As a Boro fan I hated wearing it, as you can imagine. As far as I was concerned, red and white stripes were rubbish.

That was the age when you absolutely loved playing football. For some reason the teachers used to not want you to play if it had been raining. But we were always desperate to play, whatever the weather. I can remember getting the school caretaker's brush to try to sweep away the puddles off the pitch so we could play. In fact we used to love it after it had been raining – at that age, we all felt it was even better when it was muddy and you could do slide tackles.

In my junior school days I played midfield and I used to score goals for fun. Even though I was small, I used to love a tackle. It didn't bother me how big the opposition were. In fact, my thinking was that if I hit the biggest one first then the rest would be scared of me – so I used to go flying into them.

We did have some really good players at St Pius. A few of these lads were playing for Middlesbrough Boys and went on to play for the county. I am certain some of them had trials as well. Middlesbrough seemed to be filled with these good players, that talent was different class.

Some of the lads who were a year older than me went to play for a Sunday League team called the Priory. One day my auntie came back from one of their presentation evenings and started telling me about how massive the trophies were. I am a sucker for a big trophy so that was enough for me – I immediately wanted to know where to sign up for them.

By this time I had moved up to senior school and was playing in the school team there but the idea of playing Sunday league football was totally new to me. I didn't even know pubs had football teams. As far as I was concerned, the idea of playing for two teams – the school team and the Sunday league team – was brilliant. That meant even more chance of winning more trophies, the bigger the better. I really was a trophy-hunter, me!

My secondary school was St Anthony's, which was on its own campus with three other schools below us. We used to always end up fighting with the kids from there – they used to come up the hill and we would chase them off.

For a Catholic school it had more than its fair share of bad lads. In fact, at registration the teacher would go through all the names and sometimes it was a case of, 'He's not here, sir, he's on remand ... no, he's not here either, he's in Borstal.' The teachers were tough too – they used to box your ears for fun. But if you were a decent footballer you would get away with it much more so that was great for me.

To try to get a game for the Priory, I had to meet the guy who ran the team at a place called Saltersgill, which was an estate that felt in my small world like it was about three days away from where I lived.

My dad didn't have a car and there were no buses that went that way so I had to walk. It was a real trek but when I got to the pitch there was no one else there. Not to mention the fact the grass was six inches high, which didn't impress me.

I rang him later and asked him why he had sent me to a pitch with cows on it.

But of course, it was me who had gone to the wrong pitch. They had a game without me, which he told me about in no uncertain terms in his broad Scottish accent. I could barely understand a word he was saying – he was the first of many Scots I have encountered in my football career.

He asked where I lived and what my name was. It might even have been the fact that McDermott was Scottish-sounding that swung it but this giant of a man later came round to my house.

One of the things he asked me was, 'What's your favourite Scottish team, son?' I had to say Celtic because my dad was Celtic-mad. And I sat there praying he wasn't a Rangers fan because if he was I figured that my chances of playing for Priory were gone before I had even kicked a ball.

'Good lad!' he said. 'You'll sign for me – we play in Celtic kit.'

It felt good to play in those green and white hoops. The away kit was all white like Real Madrid because he believed in the idea that it helped you to pick players out more easily.

I got invited down for a trial match the following Sunday at the same place. There was another lad there called Danny Brown who became a good mate of mine over the years. We won something like 4–0 and I think we scored two each so we both got signed up.

Soon we started to sign up various other good players from my school and one or two other schools and before you knew it we had pretty much the best of Middlesbrough Boys.

He really did have a good side. And when we signed Steve Livingstone and his twin brother Andrew we knew we were going to have a great side. They were part of a famous Middlesbrough footballing family because their dad Joe had played for Boro and was Brian Clough's understudy at one time.

We won the league and just about every cup we entered. It was a fantastic time for all of us and the great thing was we stayed together until we were 16- and 17-year-olds.

The players hardly ever changed over that time although the club itself did change. It became part of Marton FC which has gone on to produce all kinds of top players like Jonathan Woodgate, David Wheater, Lee Cattermole and Stewart Downing.

People talk about Wallsend Boys' Club in Newcastle and the number of players they have brought through over the years but I think we produced just as many – when you think of players like Phil Stamp and Stuart Parnaby as well, there has been a real production line of talent from Marton FC.

Steve Livingstone went from our club to sign for Coventry as a teenager and then he went on to Blackburn and Chelsea. In the end he came to Grimsby and stayed with us for ten years. When Grimsby first came in for him there were plenty of other clubs interested but I think what swung it for him was the fact that I was there and we were best mates who had gone back so many years.

Two school friends playing together for the same professional team, we just knew it was going to be a great craic – it was bound to be because we had a fantastic time when we started out playing together as kids in Middlesbrough.

One year, the best players from the Teesside Junior Alliance, which was the league we played in, got chosen to go to Holland for a tournament. It was an amazing experience for us because we flew there – in an actual aeroplane!

I had never even really been on a proper holiday before. For us, if you went to Whitby in a caravan for a fortnight that meant you had made it. Suddenly, here we were on a plane flying from Teesside Airport. You even got a meal during the flight – we couldn't believe it.

Mind you, it was with Dan-Air, which was one of the more cheap and cheerful airlines in those days. I think it had those propellers where you half expected that you would end up winding up the elastic band yourself so we were bricking it a bit!

In Holland they split us up and we were living with local families. That was strange enough because not only were they feeding us what we thought was dodgy food, but they also put me in with a lad from Stockton who I barely knew so he was almost as much like a stranger to me as the locals were.

The Dutch treated us really well, although they always checked to make sure our hands were clean before we were allowed to sit down for meals, which we thought was really odd.

One day they took us to Ajax Football Club to show us the skills that their lads were practising. Christ almighty, they were doing 1,000 keepie-uppies – and we could only do about three! It was another world, we just didn't do all the tricks that they were doing.

But when it came to playing them in a proper eleven v eleven game we battered them. They just weren't used to the more physical, competitive element of the game that we had been brought up on. They had all the techniques but they didn't really play eleven v eleven games at that age.

Looking back, you can see now that theirs is the right way. We were miles behind in terms of technique, even though we beat them that day. The thinking in this country was that if you were too small, forget it. You almost had to be a man even though you were still a boy if you wanted to get on.

No one worked on your technique unless you were really special and had real ability but even then your ball skills weren't really properly nurtured. You didn't get any proper coaching, unfortunately – it was much more a case of 'let's put some jumpers down and have a game of eleven v eleven'.

Playing a game of eleven v eleven is exactly what you want to do as a kid but it's not the way to develop young players and I'm afraid they're still doing things that way to a certain extent in this country.

In that sort of environment, where the physical approach seemed to hold sway, you had to be tough if you weren't the biggest, like me. But I had no fear and led by example. I think that's why I ended up as captain of most teams I played for. I took it upon myself to get stuck in and when the rest of the lads saw that, they thought they had better follow my lead.

I remember playing against Leeds Boys a few times from when I was about 12 onwards and there was a little blond lad playing for them who was a hard little bastard. His shin pads were like mine – they looked huge, like cricket pads.

The thing about him that I noticed was that when they were at home he used to get really stuck in but away from home he didn't fancy it quite so much. So I always made sure I got at him early on when he was at our place. That usually sorted him out for the rest of the game.

He was a good footballer but he was like me in a lot of ways – because of his small size he knew he had to be hard to make up for it. With him playing for Leeds, it certainly seemed to me like he had a little bit of that Billy Bremner spirit in him.

You might have guessed who I'm talking about – it was David Batty, who went on to play for England at the World Cup so he didn't do so badly for himself.

The size thing did get to me sometimes. There was one game I played in which was a county trial, Middlesbrough

Boys against Langbaurgh Boys, for the chance to play for the Cleveland county team. They had some very good players but we beat them 4–2. Steve Livingstone scored two and I got two.

At the end of the game, they sat us all down and went through the side for Saturday – and I wasn't in it. I wasn't standing for that so I piped up, 'Sorry, but you've missed my name off.'

The guy asked my name and went down the list again and said, 'No, you're not on it.' I was furious.

'Not on it? Are you kidding me? Were you watching the same game? I just scored two goals and virtually won it for you!'

But the coach said, 'The county team's about big boys, bigger than these. You'll struggle. Sorry, but it's not for you.'

I was so cheesed off, I just went home and cried my eyes out, I did, honestly. It wasn't so much that I hadn't been picked but what he had said to me. I was gutted because I started to think this was really going to hold me back in football.

My dad must have seen how upset I was so he screwed a bar across the doorway at home and had me doing stretching exercises! It sounds funny now but I was prepared to try anything to see if it worked. So I would be there hanging from it for ages. I didn't grow at all but I ended up with the longest arms in town! I looked like a monkey – my arms could reach down to my shins.

I had the bright idea of doing it the other way round hanging off it by my feet but my dad soon pointed out that was no good because the blood would just rush to my head.

We tried everything, all kinds of other ways of trying to get me to grow a bit – stretching exercises up on my tiptoes, drinking stout, eating steaks, you name it. It must have cost my mam and dad a fortune. But nothing worked. I had a metabolism like a greyhound – whatever I ate just went flying straight off me again and I certainly didn't grow any taller.

It was a big disappointment that I didn't get in the county team but looking back, none of those lads in that group made it as a pro apart from me and Steve Livingstone. I suppose that shows that your ability does come through in the long run more than the size you are.

Now that I'm coaching, when I pick a side, I make sure I pick the best players regardless of size. People sometimes try to tell me the best players are not always the right players if they're not big enough but I won't accept that. No matter how big he is, if he's good enough, he'll get in.

It happens in league football even to this day. Teams, especially in the lower divisions, go for brute strength, pace and physique. They often play from back to front and think they can manage without having any football-playing midfielders in the centre of the pitch so they go for power-houses instead.

That approach to the game was very worrying for me when I was still a schoolboy. And when my mate Steve Livingstone was signed up by Coventry, I was starting to think that my size could really prove to be an obstacle if I wanted to make it in football.

# 2

# A Saveloy For A Nose

One day, our teacher called me in and told me a guy called Jimmy Mann was interested in me. He was the chief scout for Grimsby Town at the time and he was based in Billingham, not far from Middlesbrough. Jimmy was an old guy who looked like Michael Foot, the Labour politician. You couldn't see his eyes because of his long white hair.

As soon as I found out that they wanted to offer me schoolboy forms, that was it, I wanted to sign straight away. I didn't care where it was – Grimsby might have been Timbuktu for all I cared.

The teacher asked me if I at least wanted to know where Grimsby was but when he told me it was near Hull I was still none the wiser. The next day he showed me on a map where it was but that didn't really help me either because I didn't have any idea of the scale of the map. It looked like it was just round the corner, maybe half an hour away.

'What bus do I need to get then, sir?' I asked him. He looked amazed.

'You won't be getting a bus, son. It's 130 miles away!'

My dad didn't drive so he had to get my Uncle Billy to take us down. I remember driving along the M180, which is the motorway that takes you over towards Grimsby, and it sounded like we were on an airport runway. What a racket it made – it was supposed to be a temporary surface but it stayed like that for years and years.

We pulled into a place just outside Grimsby called Weelsby Woods, not knowing that that would be the place where I would end up running my socks off in pre-season every year. My dad turned round and said to me, 'You can go home, you know. We can just turn round and drive back.'

He must have taken a look at me and thought I was in a bit of a state of shock about doing this. But I just said, 'Dad, I've come to sign. I'm not bothered about going home. I want to stay here.'

I met Dave Booth, the manager, who got me to sign the forms, and I was thrilled. I was so naïve though, I thought I was going to play in the first team that Saturday.

He told me he would show me my digs next – but that was more new territory for me. 'Digs? What do you mean, digs?' I asked. That's how wet behind the ears you are sometimes when you are only a young lad. He rolled his eyes at me and explained that I was going to live with a landlady on the seafront, which sounded good to me.

But when they first took me down there, my first impressions weren't so great. The sea was so brown it just looked like mud. But then again, I reasoned that it was the same colour as the sea at Redcar so maybe that wasn't a bad thing.

My digs were absolutely freezing, mind you, even though it was supposedly the summer – I slept in my clothes that first night!

The next day they sent one of the lads from the club to take me down to the ground. He was wearing really tight shorts, as was the fashion in those days; he had a rugby top on and flip-flops. To me, he just looked really cool – all I could think was, 'I really want to look like that. If that's what a footballer is, I definitely want to be one.' Looking back, I now realise he looked like a right plonker.

I was introduced to the assistant manager, Peter Grotier, who was a goalkeeper and would occasionally play in the first team. Pete was one of the funniest guys I have ever met in my life. He could have done stand-up comedy, he was so hilarious. In fact, he reminded me of a white version of Richard Pryor.

He took me into the manager's office to show me around and it was really impressive to someone like me. It was all wood-panelled and there was a picture of Bill Shankly on the wall. Bill Shankly, the legendary Liverpool manager! He had been Grimsby's manager back in the 1950s but it was things like that which made it feel to me that this was the big time.

Quite early on I met the physio John Fraser – what was it with these guys with a broad Scottish accent? They seemed to be everywhere in my football career. One day not long after I had arrived, I was in the shower with the lads and he got talking to me but I couldn't understand a word he was saying. All I did was nod my head – he could have been calling me every name under the sun and I was just agreeing with him.

He realised after a while that I couldn't make head nor tail of what he was saying so he sent me out to get him some talc – but I even misheard that and came back with a towel!

'What the hell's that?!' he said.

'It's a towel, like you asked for.

'No, I wanted talc!

'Yes, I know, that's what you said – a towel!'

I was so nervous that first week I actually hated it. I wasn't homesick but I was just so in awe of everything. Suddenly I was not only away from home but I was living in a man's world, with everyone effing and blinding. I had never heard language quite like that before in my life.

Really, that first stint down in Grimsby was too much for me – it was a shock to the system for me at that age. But I sat down and said to myself, 'Do I really want this?'

And the answer was, 'Yes, of course, I've got to go through with this.'

The second time I went down it was a little bit easier. They told me to bring a shirt and tie because the season had started by now for the first team and I was expected to do various duties with them.

When the full-time whistle went, the main job for us was to get in the dressing room and normally just to bring the baskets out, great big baskets for the kit to go in, and get out again.

We had already brought the tea down by then, huge pots of tea – everyone seemed to drink tea in those days. And everyone seemed to smoke as well. A cup of tea and a fag, that's what you had! It was like *Gorillas in the Mist* sometimes in that dressing room. I'm sure Kevin Drinkell and Nigel Batch used to get through twenty fags each.

One of the first times I was doing this job with the baskets, I suddenly realised the first team were already coming down the tunnel. I wasn't supposed to be still in their dressing room but I couldn't get out.

The physio came in and said, 'What are you doing in here? Quick, get in there, before the manager comes in.'

I wasn't supposed to be still hanging about in the dressing room – I should have gone into the boot room to wait then it would be my job to get the kit in and take it to the cleaners.

So the physio shoved me into what turned out to be the drying cupboard. It was basically like a sauna where they used to put the wet kit to dry. I was wearing what I thought was really smart gear. I had just been to Topman and bought myself a leather tie, six quid it was, which was a lot of money back then. I thought it was absolutely mint.

I thought I would only be hiding in there for a few minutes but they obviously hadn't played very well because Dave Booth was really laying into the players with his assistant manager Chris Nicholl. They seemed to be particularly having a go at Paul Agnew, the left-back.

After about an hour, Dave paused for breath and I assumed he had finished so I just thought to myself, 'I've had enough of this, I can't stand it any more.' I fell out of the cupboard and more or less collapsed into the kit basket in front of me.

The manager looked at me in disbelief and said, 'Who on earth's this?' But all the rest of the lads absolutely burst out laughing, I must have looked such a sight.

My hair was like a pineapple because it was a little bit dry on the top but the rest of it was so sweaty it was just stuck to my head. My shirt was drenched and I had a damp mark on the front of my grey trousers which made it look like I had wet myself.

But the worst thing of all was my tie. My precious tie had shrunk from being twelve inches long to dicky bow size! It was all dried up, peeled and cracked. I was mortified.

They even had me in the medical room to get me to recover because I had more or less collapsed. What an introduction to first team football! For days afterwards, every time someone from the club walked past me they would say, 'Look, there's that kid with the really small tie.'

And if that wasn't enough, it was the only decent shirt and tie I had with me and I hadn't got any money to buy any new gear so I had to carry on wearing it until I went back to Middlesbrough.

The third time I went down to Blundell Park, I got picked to play for Grimsby Town Colts which was the level below the youth team. I was there for two weeks this time and we had a game against a team from the North East. I knew a few of the lads from the other team because they were from my neck of the woods.

As it happened we beat them 2–1 and I got the winner from a free kick. A couple of other lads from our team – Chris Grocock and Marcus Newell – were hovering over it, arguing over who was going to take it. They were talking about trying to bend it in this way or that way, and I just said, 'Bend it? See that gap there? I'm just going to drill it into that bottom corner.'

They didn't believe me, to put it mildly, so I just shoved them out of the way and hit it straight in like an arrow. I could really ping it in those days! Before I had a chance to say 'told you!' Chris and Marcus were jumping all over me celebrating and that was the start of a good friendship between us.

With about two minutes left, one of the opposition burst through so I tripped him to stop him having a chance of equalising. Back then you could pretty much get away with taking someone out and only get a talking to rather than a yellow card.

He went flying and was fuming as he got up so we had a few words with each other. That just seemed to make it worse because by talking to me he could tell I was from the North East and they couldn't understand what I was doing playing down here in Grimsby.

Chris Nicholl was watching the game and came up to me afterwards. He said, 'That was a good goal you scored there. But do you know what I liked best? The way you took that lad out at the end with that last-ditch tackle. That showed you really wanted to win – win at all costs.'

Chris was still playing as a centre-half at that stage in his career as well as being assistant to Dave Booth. He went on to be manager at Southampton after that.

But what a hard bastard he was! He had a nose that looked like a saveloy sausage that someone had just bent in half and stuck in his face. He would shout at Andy Moore, 'You're too good-looking for a centre-half! You need your nose to be broken two or three times and have no teeth.'

Chris had a big beard on him and was a big six-footer so he looked as hard as nails. I was in awe of him. He had played for top clubs like Aston Villa and been to the World Cup with Northern Ireland. It was great for me to have him come up to me after the game.

There was another colts game early in the second week so I was hoping that if I got picked for that and played well again I might have a chance of being chosen for the youth team game at the end of my second week.

I had gone to Grimsby with another lad from the North East, a guy called Alex Gregorious from Billingham, who was a good player, quite quick. When it came to the day of the second colts game, the two of us were called over: Alex was told he was playing for the colts and I wasn't.

I was just coming to terms with that and trying to work out why I had been overlooked when Chris then hit me with the big whammy, 'You're not playing for the colts because you're playing for the reserves.'

The reserves! Forget the youth team – I had bypassed that completely and gone straight into the ressies! I was only a young lad and I was going to be rubbing shoulders with players like Paul Emson, Tony Ford and Steve Foley.

Steve was a Scouse lad, a real livewire who went on to play for Sheffield United and he was one of those players I was just in awe of. He had the biggest thighs I have ever seen. They say Mark Hughes had big thighs but, honestly, these were like tree trunks.

Andy Moore was involved in the reserves at that time too, another player I was in awe of. He was part of a real foot-balling family – his brothers Kev and Dave also played for Grimsby and their father and uncle both played for the club too in their day. Andy was hard but a good player. Even now if I see him I'm still scared of him.

Steve told me before the match, 'You stay next to me and just listen to what I tell you. If you do what I tell you, you'll be fine,' and that's what I did.

They put me on the right wing for the game, which was against York Reserves at Blundell Park, but we were losing 1-0.

Paul Emson, who really was rapid, went flying forward on the opposite wing but I was quite quick too and when he put over a cross to the far post I just remember running in and smashing it in with my head.

I simply couldn't stop scoring! It seemed like I was getting a goal every game for Grimsby at whatever level I was play-ing at. The lads were jumping all over me and it was the best feeling I had ever felt.

This was the first time I had played in a stadium like that rather than on a park pitch and it was my first ever senior goal. There were probably about 100 people there in the crowd but it might as well have been 100,000 as far as I was concerned. I had never played in front of any sort of a crowd before.

I really remember coming out of the tunnel for the first time and thinking, 'This is what I want. Imagine what it must be like when it's full. This is where I want to play – in this stadium.'

It's a good stadium, Blundell Park. Certainly in those days it was one of the nicest grounds around at that level – and I loved it.

The next day I got the local paper and there was a big headline, 'Triallist earns Town a point.' I have still got that cutting in my mam's house.

All the lads were buzzing because in the reserves you got a £2 bonus for a draw. Unfortunately I didn't get it because I wasn't getting paid. Shame really, I could have done with that two quid – I could have put it towards buying another tie.

After the game, the manager pulled me to one side and asked me if I would like to come back on a YTS, which was the Youth Training Scheme. That was the moment when I finally realised I was going to make it in football.

It was everything I had dreamed of – and it meant I could go back and stick two fingers up to the careers adviser from school who had told me I had no chance of making it as a footballer.

I have a lot to thank Dave Booth and Chris Nicholl for because I had my own doubts about whether I was big enough but they threw me in at the deep end – and I had handled it.

Maybe luck had something to do with it and maybe I was in the right place at the right time. I could have had a stinker and been bullied out of the game but I believed if you wanted it enough, you would make it happen, which is what I did.

When I rang my dad afterwards, I was absolutely full of it, telling him, 'You'll never believe it! I played for the reserves and scored – I got the equaliser! And now they've offered me a YTS as well!'

Going home, I was like a Cheshire cat.

# 3

# Bullies

Steve Livingstone and I were both buzzing about getting a club – he had been signed by Coventry, remember, so we had both taken our first steps towards being professional footballers.

But after a while the daunting prospect hit me that in a few days' time I was moving to Grimsby – to live this time, at the age of 16. Coming downstairs with my two suitcases, it was quite a big moment for me, even though I was going to stay with the same landlady on the seafront who I already knew from before.

We went straight into pre-season training when I got back to Grimsby and Jesus, it was like joining the army. Weelsby Woods really came back to haunt me – we never seemed to be away from the place.

And my competitive streak didn't do me any favours. Dave Booth would tell us to go and do a lap around the woods and my reaction would be, 'I want to win that.'

Instead of pacing myself, I would be jostling to get to the front as if it was a really important race. One time, one of the first teamers gave me a forearm smash right across the nose as if to say, 'What do you think you're doing? Get back and don't take the piss.'

He told me: 'Use your loaf, son, you'll burn yourself out. Don't get in front of us.' But I just thought, 'Bollocks, I'll beat you!' And I did on that first lap, not knowing there were another three laps to go after that.

Then they got us doing stretches and all I could think was, 'What's all this about?'
When I was a kid, all you wanted to do was throw your jumper down and start smashing balls at the goalkeeper. We never did any warm-ups.

But after a while I even got competitive with stretches, trying to stretch further than anyone else. They really put us through our paces but by the end of it I was as fit as a butcher's dog. My biggest problem wasn't anything to do with coping with the training – it was the other lads who were YTs.

Quite a few of them were from Grimsby and some from Lincoln and I thought they would be a good bunch. But most of them were bullies and they made my life hell. When I say they were bullies, I don't mean physically, I mean mentally.

Obviously it was a competitive environment and everyone was after the same thing, getting a contract, so to a certain extent it was understandable for people to want to be looking after number one.

But they didn't need to do what they did – some of them were good footballers and were going to make it anyway. I won't name names because they will know who they were. One of them came up to me later on in my football career and actually apologised. He was only a young lad at the time, the same age as me, and he was alright on his own but once he got in with the others, he would join in with them. They would come right up to me and shout abuse in my face, trying to belittle me and knock my confidence.

Perhaps they didn't realise they were doing it but they certainly destroyed my confidence. I could easily have gone home – and I'm sure lesser lads who have suffered the same kind of bullying have thrown in the towel and given up.

You only had to make the slightest mistake and they would rip the piss out of you. They would torture you with it and it wasn't nice. In fact it was so bad I used to dread going into training with them, which wasn't like me at all because I have always loved football, whether it was training or playing in a game.

I hated that first year so much that I pretty much stayed in every night and saved all my money up. The lads only invited me to go out with them once but I never went again.

There was one lad in particular who was a year older than me and would push and shove me near the kit cupboard. Yet years later when we were both pros I came across him and he was as nice as pie. He shook my hand and probably didn't think looking back that he had done anything wrong.

I only played a handful of junior games that year, deservedly so because I knew I hadn't played well enough. But it must have been linked to how much I had hated being there and how much it had knocked my confidence. My football had actually gone backwards because of the bullying.

...

Dave Booth had resigned only a few months into my first year as a YT and been replaced as manager by Mick Lyons, who had come in from Sheffield Wednesday. He had brought with him Terry Darracott who had played with him at Everton.

As far as I could see, it was Terry who was the real organiser in that team. He helped Mick a great deal. Terry was a great coach – he loved his head tennis and he absolutely hated losing. Unfortunately I was rubbish at head tennis. Whenever I got put on his team, I could hear the ball going smack on his big, bald head and then when it came to me, if I gave away a point I didn't even have to turn to look at him – I could feel his eyes boring into the back of my head.

Terry wasn't there for long and when he left, they brought in Don O'Riordan who had played for Middlesbrough so he was something of an icon to me. He turned out to be a top man and was brilliant with me, just like a lot of the other pros were at the club. I also got on really well with the schoolboys who were younger than me – in fact we had a great craic together when they were in. It was just the other YTs who were horrible to me.

I found myself in the position of having to prove myself again to the new manager. I had played for the reserves that one time and impressed Chris Nicholl but he had gone by now and Mick Lyons had his own ideas. Mick loved running, which I was good at, and he also loved his weights. Under him we were all really put through our paces. I think you could have put us in the SAS after what he had us doing.

When we got to the end of the season, all the YTs were called in and told one by one that they had been released. I was jumping for joy, I tell you – I thought they had all got what they deserved. All I needed now was for the club to offer me a deal because I really got on with the younger lads coming in and wanted to stay. I knew I could do it if I got the chance to stay on and not have to put up with the bullying any more.

But when it was my turn, Mick Lyons uttered the dreaded words, 'Sorry, son ...' I wasn't even listening any more by the time he got to the reasons why. I remember just kicking the carpet. I had a lump in my throat and I could have cried my eyes out there and then.

I wasn't bothered about what he was trying to tell me, I knew it was because he thought I wasn't strong enough even though he was saying it was because of the club's finances. I was just devastated. Part of me knew this was coming because to be a first-year pro you had to be playing in the reserves and I was nowhere near the reserves.

But the worst thing was the thought of having to go home and tell my mam and dad – not to mention Steve Livingstone had now got a pro deal with Coventry.

I still had a week to go before I was supposed to finish but Mick told me I could leave straight away seeing as I was being released. Training had finished and only the ground-staff would be left.

I told him I had come for the year so I would stay and do the full year. I was not going to leave early. In truth, it was because I just couldn't face going home so I was putting things off.

For that final week I was joined by two of the new lads who were coming the following year and the three of us spent our time working on the pitch. The other two were Tim Harvey and Marcus Newell but the strange thing was that Tim was my age and I couldn't work out how he had managed to get a YT. As we were shovelling 70 tons of topsoil onto the pitch I found out that there was now a new two-year YT and he was coming to Grimsby on the second year of his. This was something I just hadn't known about before.

When I went over to collect my last pay from a guy called Bernard Fleming, who was the secretary, he started to ask me how I was getting home because he was also from Middlesbrough originally.

'I'm going up at the weekend so I can give you a lift if you like,' he said. 'What was the reason they gave for why you were being released?'

I told him it was mainly for financial reasons and he said he couldn't understand why they hadn't thought about offering me another year as part of one of the new two-year YTs.

When Bernard asked if I would be interested in that, I nearly bit his hand off! 'Are you kidding? I'd pay them! Just give me another year!' I said.

'Just leave it with me,' he replied.

After another half an hour of shovelling topsoil, the manager waved me over. At first I thought he wanted me to make him a cup of tea but instead he called me in and said, 'You've been a good grafter, I'll give you that, son. Your attitude's been brilliant.'

Maybe it was the fact that I had opted to stay on that extra week and do some hard manual labour rather than go home early with my tail between my legs but he offered me another year.

Timber! I nearly fainted. I almost had to pick myself up off the floor before saying, 'Do I want another year? Yes, please!'

The season was over but I was so excited I couldn't wait, I didn't want to go home – I just wanted to start again straight away.

And when it did come round to my second year as a YT, it was like they had signed a different person. As well as having put the problems of bullying behind me, I was also physically in great shape. I had Don O'Riordan doing weights with me one-to-one every day, I did sprint work – I made sure I was really sharp.

And it really paid off because not only did I play the full season in the reserves and the youth team but I also got voted Young Player of the Year and broke into the first team, playing thirteen games in the Second Division [now the Championship].

That's the kind of turnaround that can happen in football over a year.

• • •

That year, no player in the youth team was ever allowed to be a bully. I'm not saying I started that all on my own, but I was one of a group of us who started it. Several of us had suffered from it ourselves in the past and we just weren't going to stand for it any more. We would have a joke and take the mickey but we wouldn't allow people to be bad-mouthed by others. If anyone went too far they got pulled up on it.

And that attitude among the players was something that eventually went all the way from the youth team right up to the first team in the time that I was at the club.

As far as I'm concerned, that's why that club had success over that period, because those lads were all together. There were no piss-takers, that kind of thing just wasn't tolerated. It was like a pact that we all made together.

Generally, you might see togetherness in a first team if they're doing well but what you don't see is such togetherness in the youth team where it's usually a case of everyone looking after themselves. But we didn't think that way – we thought, 'If we do well, we'll all get a deal. Why can't we all get a contract?'

To be fair, we weren't far wrong! From that youth team, several of us played in the first team in the same year. The likes of myself, Mark Lever, Geoff Stephenson and Tommy Watson and others all got on well in football from having been in that side.

Marcus Newell was the one player, for me, who should have made it through to the first team from that youth team but didn't. If he had done, the club would have had a hell of a player.

Alan Buckley made a mistake with him, in my opinion. Marcus was very similar to him – they played in a very similar way, both were good finishers and they even looked alike.

Marcus scored a lot of goals for the reserves and they were in the top league, up against some really good sides. In fact, they often used to get bigger crowds for the reserves than the first team if they were playing Manchester United or someone like that. They might get something like 3,500.

I remember Marcus dinking a goal over Neville Southall, the Welsh international keeper, when they were playing Everton Reserves in front of a decent crowd and I was quite envious because the first team were often only playing in front of quite sparse crowds when we were playing smaller teams like Shrewsbury.

Mind you, we had a decent crowd and a decent atmosphere for my first team debut. It was Bradford City away, in February 1987. I had just turned 18 and I couldn't believe it when Mick Lyons told me I was playing. I just thought I was making the trip to put the kit out.

Even on the Friday, I just trained as normal with the youth team, I wasn't with the regular first team players. At one point I was watching the seniors as they were doing some crossing and shooting. I had a bit of a dig at Mick because he was having a stinker at crossing the ball.

He called over to me, 'You think you can do any better, do you? Come over here and show us then!' So I did. The first one I pinged over was right on to Mick's forehead and he banged it in.

'Do you want me to do it again just to show you it wasn't a fluke?' I asked. I whipped another cross over and again it was straight on to his nut. 'Right, you can clear off back over there now with the other youth teamers,' said Mick.

I could hear him giggling to the others, 'Eighteen, he is! An 18-year-old kid talking to me like that – who does he think he is?'

My attitude must have impressed him somehow because it wasn't long afterwards that he called me in and told me, 'You're playing tomorrow on the right wing so just get your head round it.'

Bradford City had some really good players in their team that season, people like Stuart McCall, John Hendrie and Ian Ormondroyd, whose nickname was Big Stix, so it was quite a big game for me to make my debut. But I had so much confidence at the time that I took it in my stride.

Kev Moore was our skipper at that time. He was a top man and it was a terrible shock to hear he had died aged just 55 after suffering from dementia. He used to go round the back of the stand with me, Mick Lyons and his brother Andy and they had this routine that involved two boards on an angle. They had a piece of rope with a ball on it which they would throw and you would have to run, jump in the middle of the boards, head the ball, hit one board with it and then power back and hit the other one.

The two Moores were absolutely brilliant at it so it was a bit intimidating for me when they started getting me to do it. At my height I thought I would have no chance of heading it like them at first.

But, do you know what? I soon got to be able to do it as well. They were challenging me to improve that part of my game and I had a good spring. Tall players might have a natural height advantage when it comes to heading but you have got to know how to get off the floor as well. A lot of it is to do with technique and some of the tallest players aren't necessarily the best headers of the ball, maybe because they have never really felt the need to work at it.

The best header of the ball I have ever come across was David Speedie. No one used to mark him at corners because he wasn't the tallest, the defenders would all have an eye on someone else like Cyrille Regis and then Speedie would jump above them all and bang it in.

Kev said to me as we were getting ready for the game, 'Whatever you do, just carry on doing what you do for the youth team. Don't try to play differently or do what you think you should be doing for the first team. Just do what you do normally.'

As he was telling me that, I realised what a good piece of advice that was and I thought to myself that I would say the same to younger players if the situation was ever reversed. And as I got older I did find myself passing it on and I still do today.

It just goes to show what a nice guy Kev was. Here was the first team skipper pulling me to one side as we were going down the tunnel and taking the time to help me through my debut.

What made it even more special was that it was only half an hour earlier that I had poured orange juice all over him. I was so nervous I tipped it all over in the pre-match build-up!

I can distinctly remember the very first pass that I received in the match. It came from our right-back out to me on the right wing and I was being closed down by the Bradford left-back. I lifted my foot to trap it and typically it went straight underneath my foot. But amazingly, by doing that, I totally wrong-footed my marker and ran round him. Our lads must have been looking at me in astonishment because it seemed like a great bit of skill whereas in truth I had just got lucky.

I whipped the ball in and Mick Lyons met it smack in the centre of his forehead. It was like deja vu from training and in fact he should have scored from it but it was cleared off the line.

We had taken quite a decent away following to Valley Parade and from that moment on I seemed to develop a great rapport with our fans. To start with, they must have been looking at the teamsheet and thinking 'who the hell's this guy?' but very soon after I had nutmegged their left-back and put in that cross, they actually started singing my name. As soon as that started, I really thought I had made it. I thought I was the dog's bollocks, believe me!

My memories of a lot of the rest of that game are a bit hazy, to be honest, probably because I was away with the fairies. I do know we lost 4–2 but I don't think I would have really cared that much if it had been 10–0 because I was loving it so much. I was making my debut and I couldn't have been happier. I was on such a high. There was a good crowd there, well over 8,000 and I was buzzing.

That was in February 1987. What had almost gone unnoticed from my point of view was the fact that the team had actually started to drop down towards the relegation zone after a good start to the season. I was oblivious to it in lots of ways because I wasn't taking any notice of the tables. I was just enjoying being part of the first team so I didn't care about that. From the time of my debut we had something like fifteen games left and I just wanted to play in as many of them as possible.

I did play in most of them but we didn't win many and, almost unnoticed, we got dragged into a real relegation battle.

# 4

# Morning, Sergeant Major

When we were apprentices, you wouldn't believe how strict things were. It was nothing like it is now. I think these days the young lads that get signed on by big clubs get right through to playing in the first team without ever having to clean a pair of boots.

In my first year, I was assigned to doing boots and that meant there might be twenty or more players' boots I had to look after. I had to clean them all. Of course, when Christmas came around and there was a chance of getting a tip, everyone else started claiming otherwise.

The other lads would be saying 'oh yes, I'm his boot man' or 'I'm his kit man' and all of a sudden, instead of having twenty-odd people that I might get some cash from, I only ended up with about two. That made a big difference because if you were lucky you might get a nice little twenty quid for Christmas which was well worth having when you think of the money we were on.

In the second year of your YTS it was different, you would be assigned to a certain group. I got all the staff so that meant Mick Lyons, Terry Darracott, Don O'Riordan, Dave Moore and Gordon Simmonite.

It is hard to describe how strict it was. Everything was so regimented, it was like being in the army. You had to do a whole string of jobs to keep everything clean so that it was in good enough nick for a match day. We had black tiles everywhere at Blundell Park and one of the important jobs was to polish everything until you were pretty much able to see your face in it.

Every season there would be a 'top man' appointed among us. At the end of each day when all the jobs were done, the kit was all packed away and the floors were mopped – even that sometimes needed to be done two or three times because if it came up streaky you had to do it again – the top man had to go along to the manager's office and knock on his door.

'Jobs are all done,' he would say. Then Mick would come out of his office with white gloves on and go up to any pipe he fancied. He looked like a snooker referee! He would rub his finger over the top of it – and this was the bit we would all be dreading. If there was any dust on it – and I mean any dust at all – that was it. 'Right, get back in, the lot of you,' he would shout.

And it wasn't just that pipe that had to be re-done, every single job had to be done again. You certainly learned your lesson after a couple of times of that happening because you didn't want to be there until all hours. You made sure it was done properly. We had people on top of other people's shoulders cleaning the pipework right at the top, we had to take tubes out of long light fittings and dust them – we went to extreme lengths to make sure the manager didn't catch us out. It wasn't just the changing rooms, either, it was everything – the corridors, the referee's room, dining room, you name it.

The thinking behind all this was supposedly that the manager wanted everything spotless because he didn't want any germs anywhere that might cause an infection and make people ill. Mick Lyons' idea was that if someone in the first team got ill and then the first team lost as a result, that would affect everyone in the whole club so in a way it was everyone's responsibility to look after each other.

When you did the jobs on a Tuesday, the reserves might well have a game so you would have to get everything spick and span but then the reserves would come back in after the game and the whole lot would need doing again. You would end up cleaning everything twice in the same day. We would start at half past eight in the morning and on some days we wouldn't get away until ten o'clock at night. We would have fish and chips for our tea in the kit cupboard. They were long hours to work for only £27 a week, that's for sure.

One of the tricks Mick started to do to make sure we were cleaning everything properly and weren't cutting corners was hide a piece of paper saying, 'Find me.' It might only be half an inch wide and he would hide it behind little brackets on the walls or he might poke it through into little vents where the only way you could find it was by unscrewing the fixtures and fittings. You just had to carry on screwing things off and looking into little holes until you found it – because if you didn't find it he would just say, 'Sorry, lads, there's a piece of paper there. Jobs aren't done unless you've found it.'

If you got the wrong side of him, Mick wasn't averse to getting a ruler out and knuckling you over the back of the hand like a schoolteacher. Bang! He would smack you over the knuckles and shout, 'Go and get those jobs done again.'

It got to the point where any time you walked past him you had to salute him! He wanted you to say 'morning, Sergeant Major Lyons' or 'morning, Wing Commander Darracott'. And if you had your hands in your pockets, you would be in for the high jump – you would have to do laps.

Mick Lyons had been at Sheffield Wednesday under Howard Wilkinson who was very keen on discipline and hard work so that was presumably where he got it from. Wilkinson wanted his players to run, run and run. Mick had a similar philosophy. Once when we all turned up late, he made us all go for a run in the snow through the fields after we had been in the gym and were all sweating. By the time we got back we were all absolutely solid like blocks of ice.

Things were so much stricter then, compared to now. As apprentices, if we wanted to go into the first team dressing room, we would have to knock on the door and ask politely, 'Can I come in?' If they said no, you weren't allowed in, it was as simple as that. These days that sort of thing would never happen. First teamers are more likely to go into their dressing room and find kids lounging about in their place.

Mick certainly gained your respect – in fact a lot of us were petrified of him. He was like your dad. If you stepped out of line you knew you might well end up getting battered. It wasn't just the apprentices that he was strict with, it was the first team too. Probably about half of the first teamers liked him and the other half thought he was clueless. It depended as much on whether you were playing or not rather than his methods.

As a second-year apprentice, I really admired Mick despite his strict regime. A lot of people in Grimsby don't really have a very high opinion of him even now but he gave me my big shot and I looked up to him. I can't say a bad word about the guy. He gave me confidence.

Mick did try to look after us younger lads in his own way. He once decided to kit us all out with some jackets to make us look smarter. 'I've got you all some suit jackets. They're in the back of my car, come and get one,' he said.

So we all trooped out to pick one each, thinking he had gone out and bought some new jackets for us. But when we got out to his car, our faces fell and we realised they were all his old jackets. Maybe he had been having a clear-out of his wardrobe but bear in mind that Mick Lyons was a strapping great old-fashioned central defender and we were just kids who were dwarfed by him; we all looked ridiculous wearing these things. My mate Marcus Newell got a burgundy one which was absolutely minging. Mick insisted that we wore them for matches but can you imagine what we looked like? They really were shocking, they made us look like tramps more than anything.

It wasn't just Mick who was very regimented in everything he did – it rubbed off on some of the others in senior positions at the club at that time. One of them was Dave Moore, who ran the youth team. Through the week the first team had a particular red top that they wore, except on a Friday when they weren't allowed to wear them. Now I was in charge of the matchday kit, which meant on a Friday it all had to go into the skip and be counted off to make sure we had the right number of everything. One week, it was absolutely pouring with rain and Andy and Kev Moore came over to the skip looking for some dry kit to put on.

I said, 'Sorry, you can't have those, lads.' In return, I just got the glare from both of them as if to say, 'Who are you telling us what we can and can't wear?'

Before I knew it Dave was there as well, telling them to put their kit right back in the skip. They started to protest, saying they needed dry kit because it was raining. But Dave wasn't standing for any nonsense and even though he was their own brother, he told them in no uncertain terms to put the kit back. This was Andy and Kev Moore, who I was scared stiff of – and Dave was bossing them around!

I decided there and then I was never going to mess with Dave, that was for sure.

But Dave was a brilliant guy. He went on to become manager at Scunthorpe, then he came back to Grimsby and he has done just about every job going at Blundell Park. He has been youth team manager, reserve team manager, assistant manager, manager, physio – you name it, he has done the full lot. Head physio is his most recent position at the club and it wasn't long ago that he filled in again as caretaker manager. There is no one more experienced at that club than Dave Moore. And yet even now, if I see Dave, I give him the same respect that I did when I was a 19-year-old YT because he helped me on my way and he still treats you well even though it's years later.

Dave is as hard as nails and he also has the tightest grip of anyone I have ever known. If you ever meet anyone who knows Dave, they will say the same thing, 'If you ever shake his hand, don't grip it back because the harder you grip the more he wants to break your hand.' If you keep thinking to yourself 'I'll just grip it a little bit harder', he'll crush you. He really will.

He is also the only physio I know who would sit there in December in snow, hail and sleet, you name it, even if it was minus six degrees he would still have a pair of shorts and a T-shirt on. I think his mother eventually had to have a word with him to say, 'Dave, please, put another top on.' He made me feel really cold – and, remember, I'm from the North East.

When we were playing Swansea once, I can remember everyone else was wrapped up as warm as they could get because it was so freezing but Dave was there on the bench in his usual shorts and T-shirt. After a bit we noticed he had turned blue – I mean really blue. I was on the bench as well because I was injured at the time, I had gloves on, jumpers on and I could feel the snot coming out of my nose was almost frozen solid.

When I glanced across to Dave, the colour of him was unbelievable. He was absolutely blue, he was shaking and the muscles in his legs were popping with cold. The rest of us looked at each other and were thinking, 'He's going to die of cold sitting there on that bench unless someone goes and gets him a hot drink to warm him up!' But Dave wasn't bothered, that's just how he was.

In that Mick Lyons year, all of us got really toughened up because of his regime. By the end of it, we were all massive physically because of the weights we were doing. It seemed like we did weights day and night because we were doing them three evenings a week anyway and then Don O'Riordan brought me and another lad called Chris Grocock in for extra weights every morning as well.

Chris was a young player who had done well and broken into the first team and they obviously decided they wanted to really build the two of us up. It must have worked because there's a team photo which must have been taken towards the end of Mick Lyons' time as a manager where if you look carefully I have got the biggest shoulders of anyone apart from Dave Moore. Not bad for someone who was supposed to be too small to make it as a professional footballer.

As well as toughening us up physically, the club wanted to look after us academically too so in our first year as apprentices, we had to go to college one day a week to do a City and Guilds course in sport.

My teacher was Lee Stephens, who was a monster of a guy. He was a real beast, must have been 6ft 4in, massively built, an ex-rugby player. You really didn't want to mess with him, I can promise you. But he was a top man,

I have really good memories of him. It wasn't just Grimsby Town lads who were there, it was apprentices from other clubs around the area, mainly Scunthorpe United and Hull City. At the time Hull had a particularly good youth team, just as we did. We both had a reputation for producing good young players.

There were thirteen of us in that group who went to what later became Grimsby Institute on a Thursday. I was there with another guy from Grimsby called Les Thompson. One of the players in the group was a young Dean Windass. Now if you imagine I was only 5ft 7in, Deano was a similar size to me. And he was also skinnier than me. In build, he was nothing like the player you think of in his later career. But he had great ability even at that age. His footwork was amazing, he was full of tricks.

Deano was also jack the lad, just as you would imagine. He was hilarious at college but he was always getting kicked out of class for what he said and did. He was the class clown and nothing you could do would stop him cracking jokes the whole time. He just couldn't help himself. Deano used to turn up to classes half an hour late sometimes as well because he had been into town or whatever. He found it difficult to apply himself to being in a classroom because playing football was all he ever wanted to do.

As part of our course, we all had to do a bronze medal swimming course at Scartho Baths. There was a woman called Biddy Rowe in charge who is still involved in swimming in the area to this day. I really enjoyed it because I was a good swimmer. Some of the other lads weren't bothered about it though and just wanted to get back home to Hull or Scunny. One afternoon we were doing a lifesaving technique which entailed hauling on ropes and Biddy was telling us how to do it properly.

All of a sudden we heard this voice from the very top diving board high up above us, 'Try pulling on this.' It was Deano of course, who had sneaked up on to the diving board, done a moonie and then dived into the pool.

Biddy went absolutely ballistic and threw him out there and then. Lee Stephens had to ring up Brian Horton, who was Hull's manager at the time, and tell him they had a real problem with Windass and it wasn't long after that incident at the swimming pool that Deano got booted out by his club.

It was after being released that he ended up in non-league football with North Ferriby United. But of course Hull came back for him a few years later and he went on to have a fantastic career. In fact every single one of us in that group made it as a professional footballer – even though Biddy was always telling us none of us ever would unless we knuckled down and started to do some work. She was pleased that we did make it in the end though.

About a year after the diving board prank I bumped into Deano again at Hull bus station. I hadn't seen him since and I remember he didn't have a coat on even though it was raining. He had his hands wrapped up in his jumper trying to keep them warm and when I looked at him, he just seemed like a skinny little lad.

But after he had been to North Ferriby and then got back to Hull City as a pro, the next time I saw him his physique was totally different. He had completely changed, he was huge now, not fat but just solid, with muscles everywhere. And once he had filled out like that he never looked back. He became a legend at more than one club, which isn't bad going, having the success he had at clubs like Hull and Bradford City. Deano has had his ups and downs more recently but I will always wish him good luck because he is a nice lad and his heart's in the right place.

# 5

# A Clean Pair Of Shorts

Although I made my first team debut at Bradford playing on the right wing, I very soon started to get the first few hints that the manager saw me playing in a more defensive position.

We had a right-back called Dave Burgess who was a great player and really knew how to stay on his feet. The most valuable piece of advice I ever had from him was that the best defender on any team was the one with the cleanest pair of shorts. He told me that you didn't need to go to ground and you didn't have to nail players on the other side either to be a good defender. You should always stay on your feet and you would usually be able to twist and turn and poke the ball away. It was a great piece of advice and one that I really took to heart. In some ways, that became my forte, staying on my feet rather than sliding in rashly.

Once Mick Lyons started to move me to right-back in training Dave started to get worried about his own future. Dave called me over one week in training and said, 'I've got a funny feeling he's going to pull me from the team. And if he does and you play right-back instead of me, I'm going to come into that boot room and absolutely batter you on Monday.'

Obviously he was only joking but I was still only a young lad and I thought he was being serious. After training you would get called over by Mick Lyons to be told if you were being dropped from the first team and I was just hoping and praying he wouldn't call Dave's name out as I was really worried what he would do to me if I ended up taking his place at right-back. And just as I got to the door to leave, there was a shout from Mick, 'Burgey!' I groaned quietly to myself as Dave turned to me and said, 'I'll see you Monday.'

But he was spot on with what he had worked out, the manager did pick me to play right-back that week and I had an absolute blinder. It was against Sheffield United and I could have scored a hat-trick, even though I was playing right-back. I had one cleared off the line, one that was tipped on to the crossbar and I also missed a diving header.

Full-backs in those days were expected to be at the far post for when the other guy crossed from the other side. You really had to get up and down the pitch, which seemed to suit my style of playing. I never really looked back from that day and played as an attacking right-back pretty much right up to the end of season.

One of the more memorable games – for all the wrong reasons – was an away game at Plymouth Argyle, who were doing pretty well that season. It is a massive pitch at Home Park with a slope on it, which makes it a difficult place to play.

Even getting there was a long old trek from Grimsby and to a young lad like me from Middlesbrough, it felt like the end of the earth. I ended up sharing a hotel room with the physio John Fraser. When we got there, he said to me, 'Right, I'm going out.'

I was wondering, 'What does he mean? Where's he going?' But he just said with a wink, 'If anyone asks, I've been here all evening.'

When he came back from the hotel bar he was absolutely leathered and woke me up in the middle of the night. It maybe wasn't ideal preparation for me the night before the game. But then the next morning he wanted me to go down early to the ground to help him put the kit out even though I was playing.

I didn't mind so I went down early with him. As soon as I got there, Mick Lyons pulled me over to one side and told me someone from the England Under-21s was coming to watch me that day.

He said, 'You've done great up to now, well done. So I just wanted to let you know. You're playing against this left-winger today who's not bad. He's quick but not as fast as you so don't worry, you'll nail him.'

I was absolutely buzzing about the idea of the England Under-21s being interested in me. Then he said: 'Do you know what? I fancy doing a 12-minute run. Get some kit on, you can come with me, you're a fit young lad. Come on, we'll do eight and a half laps round the pitch.'

A 12-minute run? Eight and a half laps? Round that pitch? It was absolutely huge – and half of it was uphill. That was the last thing I needed after my disturbed night's sleep.

We did the run but I was really blowing by the end so when it came to the match I was struggling. The lactic acid that had built up in my thighs was absolutely horrendous. We lost the match 5–0 and the left-winger I was up against scored a hat-trick and set up the other two. I think I must have almost got him a move to Real Madrid but I was bombed out by the England Under-21s.

The manager came up to me afterwards and said to me, 'I don't know what you've been doing today son but you just weren't at it.' I stared at him open-mouthed. This was the guy who had got me doing a 12-minute run just before the match!

The England Under-21s never came back to watch me again so that was my chance gone. You never know what might have happened if things had gone differently that day. Funnily enough that wasn't quite the only sniff I had of international football in my career. Lawrie McMenemy had a spell as Northern Ireland manager in the late 1990s and at one stage approached our physio John Fraser to find out if I was eligible to play for them through Irish ancestry.

For me personally, it was great to be a regular in the first team but as the season went on, we were more and more up against it in our relegation battle.

It came down to a game right at the end of the season at home to Hull which we really needed to win to keep alive our hopes of staying up. There was a lot at stake but I was young and enjoying it so the pressure didn't get to me. At one point, the Hull left-back came into the corner with me and I nutmegged him, which he wasn't very happy about.

He said, 'If you nutmeg me again, I'll boot you right over that stand, do you understand?' But I wasn't intimidated by stuff like that so when he came and tried to kick me a bit later in the game, I did him again with a nutmeg.

I was swaggering around after that because we were 2-0 up and the atmosphere in Blundell Park was electric. The crowd was nearly 7,000 which was a decent size for us and I was absolutely buzzing – it looked like we were staying up after all and we were beating our local rivals to boot.

Hull's manager Brian Horton was fuming with their centre-forward so he brought on a lad called Andy Saville. We weren't worried about him because although he was a decent player and quite hard with it, he didn't have a great goalscoring record at that stage of his career. We thought we were home and dry – but Saville played a blinder and scored twice. Those were the goals that sent us down.

We had one more match to go that season but to all intents and purposes, it was allowing Hull to come back and draw that game 2–2 which got us relegated. Before you knew it, there were rumours flying around that Mick Lyons was going to get the sack – and that put me in an anxious position because I was still in the second year of my YTS and had no idea whether I was going to be offered a contract if someone new came in who didn't know me.

I went to see Mick and he was very reassuring even though he probably knew he was going to get sacked. He said, 'You're going to be all right, don't worry. I'm offering you a two-year deal and I'm going to send you the contract in the post.'

That was fantastic news for me so while he was in a good mood and things were going so swimmingly I thought I'd mention something else that had been on my mind. 'Er, gaffer. You know I've played twelve games? Well, I've not been paid,' I piped up.

He asked me what I meant so I said, 'Well, I've just been getting my YT money, that's all. Don't I get any bonus or appearance money?' Mick exploded at me at that point. 'Get out of this office!' he shouted.

'Get paid? You've had the satisfaction of making your debut and playing for the first team and now you want paying for it as well? Go on, clear off!' I swear to God, I must have lifted clean off the ground as he was yelling at me.

After that, all I could think was that he would be so upset at me that he might not give me a contract after all. And at first nothing came in the post so I started to get really worried, particularly when Mick did get the sack.

But then back at home in Middlesbrough, there was the letter waiting for me. A two-year deal – and on £100 a week! I had only been on £27 before so this seemed like riches. I was going to be minted.

Mick Lyons went back to Everton coaching after he got the sack at Grimsby and the last I heard of him he was out in Brunei working in football. I haven't seen him since the day he left Blundell Park, which is a shame in a way because he was very good to me and I can't thank him enough for what he did for my career.

For the 1987/88 season, Bobby Roberts came in to take over as manager – yet another Scot. He was a lovely guy and a great coach but we just did not seem to be able to win a game under him. I played all over the pitch for him as he tried to find a winning formula – I played right-back, left-back, right-wing, left-wing, centre midfield. I even played thirteen games as centre-forward for him.

I quite enjoyed it actually, I thought I was Marco Gabbiadini. I did have plenty of pace and used to enjoy laying it off to other players like Marc North and Stevie Saunders. Northy was a good player who used to be a goal-keeper at Luton but he played up front for us because he was so quick and he ended up making a career as a striker. He sadly had to retire early because of injury and died of cancer at a very young age.

We had bags of pace between the three of us but we couldn't finish for toffee. At least, I couldn't and Stevie wasn't much better. The best we could manage was to win lots of corners so that's what we did, get corners and tried to get goals that way. To be honest, we just didn't have enough for that league.

It was another fight against relegation all season and when it came to the last game, we needed to beat Aldershot at home. It was 1–1 when we got a penalty which could have been our lifeline. Northy stepped up to take it but, honestly, it was so weak it barely reached the keeper. It stayed 1–1 and we went down again, our second relegation in a row, down to what was still the Fourth Division in those days.

I didn't play all that much that season, only about twenty games, so it was a disappointing time for me all round. But I have some funny memories of that year, nonetheless. Bobby Roberts was hilarious at times. He used to kick the living daylights out of dugouts during games because he used to get so worked up as we were playing. You should have seen the state of them afterwards, it was unbelievable, and there would be water bottles lying around everywhere. We had a good team on paper. Up front we had Scott McGarvey, who started out at Manchester United, but we just couldn't win a game.

And the more we lost the more Bobby would get furious and kick the dugout, throwing bottles around. When we lost and we went back into the dressing room, you would think to yourself, 'He is actually going to kill someone this time.' But all he would say was, 'Unlucky lads. That wasn't a bad performance today. See you Monday.' It was amazing, we couldn't believe how calm he was afterwards when he had annihilated the dugout during the 90 minutes.

Another good thing for me personally that season was scoring my first ever goal for the first team. It was away at Gillingham and they put me out on the right wing again. We were 1–0 down and when the chance came, the keeper came charging out to me to narrow the angle and try to put me off. He did give me the heebeegeebees a bit but I nutmegged him, just banged it through his legs. It was a great feeling to get the equaliser which got us a point because it finished 1–1.

The previous season I could have scored fifteen when I played those first twelve games under Mick Lyons but I didn't get any so it was brilliant to score one at last. The lads were buzzing because we had got a draw so they all got a bonus. Our away form hadn't been very good and that was the first league point we had got away from home for about three months.

The manager thought we were staying up after I scored that equaliser in February 1988 – almost exactly a year after I had made my debut at Bradford – but we never did of course. It was an awful year, all in all. In fact, it was probably the worst season I had as a pro at Grimsby.

One good thing that happened during 1987/88 was that I ended up living with John Fraser – he was the physio whose Scottish accent I couldn't understand at first, remember. I was only meant to stay there for a week but I ended up living with his family for seven years. If it wasn't for his family and also Marcus Newell's family, I don't think I would have stuck it out, to be honest. I think I would have gone back home to Middlesbrough so I owe a massive debt of gratitude to John, Nicky, Scott and Craig for everything they did for me in those years. I spent a lot of time with Scott and in all those years, we never really had a single argument. He was such a lovely lad and it was largely down to them that I really enjoyed my time at Grimsby.

One problem, however, was that we used to go out on the Friday night before the match. You would never get away with that these days – you would get kicked out. But John used to insist and before you knew it we would end up having six pints. I would get told that I wasn't in the first team the following day so the night before we would go out and I would have pasty, chips and beans but then I would find out on Saturday that I was playing after all.

Under Bobby Roberts there was one week when I was in plaster because I had done my ankle ligaments but the rule was that you still weren't allowed to go out the night before a game even if you were injured. However, John persuaded me to go out with him to a pub called the Hainton and sat me down in the lounge bar near the restaurant.

'Sit there, no one'll see you, you'll be alright,' he told me as he went off to the bar. I could see he had got two pints and was waiting for his change when I turned round and couldn't believe my eyes – Bobby Roberts and his missus had walked in to have a meal and sat down right next to me. He didn't look at me and he didn't say anything. We both just looked straight ahead. By this time, Fraz was coming back with the drinks and obviously clocked that the manager was there so he veered off into the other bar without even saying anything to Bobby either. I had no idea what to do so I got up and limped off into the other bar as well.

Fraz said, 'I can't believe it but somehow I don't think he's noticed you.' We downed the pints quickly and legged it, relieved that we had managed to get away with it. But when it came to the match the next day, during the team talk, the manager said:

You know what, Macca? I went in this pub last night called the Hainton, not far from where you live actually. And do you know what? There was a lad sat in there next to me and my missus who was the absolute ringer of you. If you've got a twin – and they always say you've got one in life – he's yours.

I just blurted out, 'Yeah, they do say that, don't they?' And then he said, 'And do you know what makes it even better? He even had a pot on the same leg!'

The lads were absolutely bursting with laughter but Bobby had got his point across and said, 'Don't let me ever see you out on the night before a game again.'

• • •

There is a theory that the key to being a successful physio is to do with timescales – and Fraz certainly had it down to a tee. No matter what was wrong with you, he would always tell you it would take six weeks to recover.

'Fraz, I've got a thigh strain,' you would say.

'Six weeks,' would be the reply.

'Hamstring.'

'Six weeks.'

'Broken my arm.'

'Six weeks.'

It didn't matter if it looked like a slight problem or a serious injury, Fraz always seemed to say it would be six weeks.

The pay-off for the physio would come when an injured player was back in training after only ten days. The manager might say, 'I thought you said that would be six weeks, Fraz?'

And quick as a flash would come the reply, 'I know boss, I'm working miracles here!'

At one point Fraz started using a new technique he had been shown which he called impact treatment. It involved using a tiny sandbag and a heavy sandbag. What he did was to get a player to lie on the treatment table, put his foot on the small sandbag and then he would drop the big one repeatedly from a great height right on his injured ankle. Players were dreading it after a while because it was so painful but we all presumed it must be doing us some good because he was the physio and he knew best.

Eventually we got a visit from someone checking how this new treatment was working. Fraz was happy to show him a demonstration so he brought in a player to lie on the treatment table – but it was our visitor who started to set up the treatment. And the first thing everyone there immediately noticed was that he put the BIG sandbag on the end of the table and rested the player's foot on it!

Dave Moore immediately glanced over the guy's shoulder and looked at Fraz as if to say, 'Have you been doing this wrong all this time?' Before he could say anything, Fraz made a signal to indicate that he would kill him if he breathed a word – and then the visitor, who actually seemed to know all about impact treatment, picked up the little sandbag and started tapping lightly it on the injured player's ankle. It took Fraz a long time to live that one down!

Don't get me wrong, Fraz was brilliant at his job but we had some hilarious times with him. He had these heat tubes which he would wrap round your legs with a towel and he would say, 'If you move, that'll burn right though your leg. It'll go right through your skin, through your muscle and burn the bone.'

Once he had said that, players would be panicking and getting terrified of being burnt if they so much as flinched. Then he would casually say, 'Right, I'm just nipping into town, I'll be back in half an hour.' Fraz was hilarious like that. Players would be petrified of getting burnt but from his point of view it was a great way of keeping players to lie still while he was out. He didn't want them wandering around the dressing room because people would then start to ask questions about where he was.

We had a player called Peter Rawcliffe who was the hairiest lad I have ever known in my life – you wouldn't believe how hairy his legs were. He had this heat tube treatment one day and Fraz did his usual routine, warning him not to move a muscle or he would risk getting burnt. And while Pete was lying there stock still, Fraz calmly got a razor out and shaved his initials PR on his leg! The letters stood out a mile because the hairs on his legs looked like they were about three inches long.

Pete started trying to object, 'Stop it! What are you doing?' But Fraz just turned to him and said, 'Don't you dare move or else you know what'll happen.'

He did all kinds of other funny stuff. Fraz loved to make the most of the fact that Blundell Park was close to the coast by taking players to the beach when they were injured. If you had an ankle ligament problem, he would have you in the sea. If it was a bad back, you would be in the sea. And he would bring apprentices down to the beach in a minibus and get them in the sea as well as part of one of his treatments.

'Go on, get in there, the saltwater's good for you,' he would say. And then he would get them collecting driftwood from the beach for him to take back home and burn on his log fire!

One day when I was living at Fraz's house but he wasn't there, I was having my tea but some of the other lads from the club had come over and were messing around in his medical room. Fraz had his own treatment room at his home and the lads shouldn't have been in there, but of course, I couldn't stop them – they were lying on his couch and generally getting up to no good. I knew we would be for the high jump if he came back and found us. Fraz used to have a massive box of crisps and he sometimes let us have a packet so as to keep the other lads quiet, I told them to take a packet of crisps and stop messing around.

Next thing you knew, Marcus Newell had grabbed as many packet of crisps as he could lay his hands on, stuffed them up his jumper and was now lying on the treatment table groaning, 'I feel sick! I've eaten too many crisps!' At that very moment, there was the sound of the key in the front door – we were well and truly rumbled.

Fraz was furious. 'What's going on here? What are you lads up to in here?' Then he saw Marcus's jumper bulging and felt all the crisps hidden under there.

'Those are my crisps! Are you lot robbing my house?' he yelled.

He counted out about fifteen bags of crisps from under his jumper and sent them packing. But that wasn't the worst of it. The next morning when Fraz saw me he still looked pretty annoyed and asked if I had enjoyed my tea.

When I said I had, he replied, 'I'm glad you did. Do you know what I had for my tea when I got in? I'll show you.'

We used to get our tea cooked for us and it would be left under one of those silver domes to keep it warm in case you were late coming back from somewhere. Fraz lifted the silver dome from his tea from the night before – and underneath there was just a folded piece of paper with 'mmmmmm' written on it. Marcus and the others had scoffed his tea as well!

Unfortunately for Marcus, he used to suffer badly from blackheads, particularly in his ears. Fraz offered to help get rid of them with a syringe and he made sure he got his revenge by making him suffer while he did it. Poor old Marcus was yelping with pain.

Fraz also liked a cigar and you would sometimes wonder where he was until you saw a big puff of smoke coming from inside the dugout – just like a scene from an advert on the telly. They don't make them like him any more.

# 6

# Harry The Haddock

Very soon after Bobby Roberts left, I got a phone call from Don O'Riordan telling me he had got the sack too. He told me he had heard there were a couple of guys who were in contention for taking over as manager but he was very clear who he thought should get the job.

'As far as you're concerned, the guy you want is Alan Buckley,' he told me. 'You'll like him. He likes his teams to play football and he'll really like you as a player. I have given him a bit of a run-down on you and told him you'd fit in really well with how he likes to play.'

I was grateful to Don for putting in a good word for me and after what he had said about Alan Buckley, I was really pleased when I heard that it was Alan who had got the job. But then some of us started to dig a little deeper into Alan's managerial career and realised his most recent club had been Kettering Town, who were in the Conference. Suddenly, I was thinking to myself: 'Non-league? Does that mean he'll take us down into non-league as well?'

When it came to the first day of pre-season, there were only about six of us left. Everyone else was gone – released or shipped out to other clubs. We were just coming to terms with how few of us there were and scratching our heads over that when this guy we didn't recognise came down the corridor. My first impression of him was that he looked just like Roger De Courcey, the comedian who did Nookie Bear. He was only a small fellow but he had a bit of a strut about him. I was just coming out of the boot room and said good morning to him.

I'll always remember the first words that he said to me, 'Good morning? What's good about it? You've just been relegated.' And that was my very first conversation with Alan Buckley. I thought, 'Oh my god, I'm finished! I'm not going to like this fella.'

But my first impressions of him were so wrong, looking back. In that first year that he was in charge, he brought in lots of new players. That was not a surprise as there were so few of us to start with, and quite of few of them were from his old club Kettering, people like Andy Tillson and Paul Reece. Some of the other new arrivals were Keith Alexander, who came from Barnet, and John Cockerill from Stafford Rangers.

As well as those non-league recruits, he brought in some lads he knew from Walsall like Gary Childs and Richard O'Kelly. Grimsby also had some good players left from the Bobby Roberts era, like goalkeeper Steve Sherwood who had played in the FA Cup Final for Watford. There were also Shaun Cunnington, Kevin Jobling and Chris Hargreaves and he brought in Steve Stoutt from Wolves so you could see we had the nucleus of a decent squad.

Alan Buckley brought in so many players that to start with a lot of us didn't really think we would gel together as a squad. In fact, in the early days you could almost sense there was a bit of a divide, particularly between the non-league lads who all more or less knew each other and the half a dozen of us who were left from the previous manager. A lot of the new apprentices who came in were from the Nottingham area too rather than local Grimsby lads.

And Alan had brought Arthur Mann in with him who had a lot of contacts in and around Nottingham and Mansfield.

One of the first things that happened under Alan and Arthur was that they totally got rid of the youth team and just decided to concentrate on the first team and the reserves, with Alan running the first team and Arthur in charge of the reserves. Arthur was just about the fittest guy I have ever come across in my life. He had already been retired from playing for quite a few years after quite a lot of success with clubs like Manchester City, Notts County and Mansfield. He was still fit enough to have been playing. Sadly Arthur died a few years later following an industrial accident otherwise I think he would still have been fit enough to be kicking a ball about today.

We hated it when Arthur took us on runs around Weelsby Woods because he was fitter and faster than the rest of us. He was like a whippet! And in those days Alan used to join in training too. Although we didn't know too much about him as a manager, he had been a really good player in his day. In fact he was a bit of a legend at Walsall, where he spent most of his playing career. Alan is one of Walsall's all-time leading goalscorers and when he left the club briefly for a spell at Birmingham they bought him back for a club record fee of £175,000.

When he joined in training sessions, that was when we realised what a good player he had been – but he was also a really hard task-master. If you were on his side in a practice match and you passed it to him just half a foot either side of him, he would be effing and blinding at you.

'Give it to my feet! How can I score a goal if you don't give it to my feet – that's no good to me,' he would shout.

Early on, Alan pulled me to one side and told me he thought I was too big and wanted to slim me down. In fact, he thought we had all done far too much in the way of weights, which meant we were too bulky and not fit enough. What he did with us in training pretty much the whole time was shuttle runs and games of eight versus eight, nine versus nine, eleven versus eleven. And he did get us all much sharper and quicker on the pitch.

Don O'Riordan was right – Alan certainly liked to play a passing game. That was what Alan drummed into us right from the start; pass the ball, pass the ball, pass and follow. But it took him quite a lot of tinkering with the team to begin with before he got us how he wanted. To start with he played me as a left-winger, which was a position I had hardly ever played before in my life. I think I lasted about 45 minutes playing out there at Cambridge away in the first league game of the 1988/89 season. He wouldn't let me play there after that and I'm not surprised.

I switched over to the right wing, which was more my natural side at least, and then when Tommy Wright was injured, Alan moved me back to right-back for a game away at Hereford. I knew I could do that job because when I played for Mick Lyons I was strong and fit but now I had become a lot sharper and quicker because of all the running work we had done. It meant if anyone did beat me, I was fast enough to get back and recover, which is a great asset for a defender. I had a great game at Hereford so Alan put me in there again the following game and from there I never really looked back. From that point on I was a right-back and it was Alan Buckley who had properly found what my best position was.

I was encouraged to keep it simple. What Alan told me was to get the ball and give it to Gary Childs, who was playing in front of me. It does sound simple but it really worked because I built up a great understanding with Childsy. We had a decent season in the league under Alan in 1988/89 but we didn't quite have enough about us to mount a proper promotion challenge. We finished ninth, just outside the play-offs, which made a nice change for those of us who had experienced relegation two years in a row.

After the struggles we had had in recent seasons, it felt good to be a bit higher up in the league and playing such good football as well, even though we missed out on promotion. But the most memorable aspect of that first season under Alan Buckley was our fantastic FA Cup run which took us to within a whisker of the quarter-finals.

First we beat Wolverhampton Wanderers, who were in the Third Division in those days but had some really good players like Steve Bull and ended up winning their league that season. Then we knocked out Rotherham United, who went on to be Fourth Division champions as well so that was two nice scalps for us early on in the competition. Beating Rotherham got us through to the third round proper when the big clubs join in.

We drew Middlesbrough away which was fantastic for the Mariners because Boro were in the top flight at the time but also perfect for me personally because it was my home patch.

It was January 1989 when we went up to Ayresome Park and I was absolutely desperate to win of course, especially because I knew all my mates were there in the crowd. Middlesbrough actually struggled in the league that season and ended up getting relegated on the last day by losing at Sheffield Wednesday. But up until we played them in the FA Cup in January they had been doing OK. They had some terrific players like Tony Mowbray, Gary Pallister, Colin Cooper, Stuart Ripley, Peter Davenport and Bernie Slaven and there was a crowd of nearly 20,000 packed into the ground so we were really up against it, particularly when Bernie put them 1–0 up in the first half.

The week before, Boro had beaten Manchester United, which just shows what we were up against, but Marc North came on as a substitute in the second half and scored two goals to knock them out. The first one was a long throw by Kevin Jobling which Keith Alexander won in the air against Pallister for Northy to bang it in. And then those three were involved again with only a few minutes left; Kev crossed it, Keith headed it backwards over their keeper and Northy just managed to squeeze a header home. Even then, Boro might have equalised right at the death; Bernie Slaven lobbed our keeper Paul Reece but I managed to run back and head it off the line.

It was a real onslaught, one of the toughest games I have ever played in. We had to throw bodies on the line and I lost count of how many corners they had but Paul had a brilliant game in goal. The last 15 minutes felt like three-quarters of an hour because conditions underfoot were heavy and Ayresome Park was a massive pitch so we were naturally tiring towards the end.

It was a fantastic result for us but it was pandemonium for me after the game. I was getting messages from all my friends saying, 'You'd better not be coming out in the Boro tonight. You're dead if you do!' They were threatening to batter us if we dared to show our faces. After the game I thought I had better keep my head down so I went out with a few friends to a local pub we knew in Middlesbrough called the Jack and Jill where we thought we would be nice and safe.

But after a while someone brought in a copy of the local paper and opened it to the sports pages so I was immediately diving for cover when I saw the headlines. 'Quick, shut that paper up, there's a photograph of me in there tackling one of the Boro players!' I was yelling.

Bernie Slaven was a legend, a real Boro hero of mine growing up, a hero to all of us who watched Boro when we were kids so it was a great feeling to be playing against him. I would be at the Holgate End watching him as I was growing up and when Bernie scored, I would be one of the fans running up towards the pitch and shaking the fence in celebration. At the time I would have done anything to be able to jump over that fence and join in the celebrations – and now here I was playing against him.

Beating Middlesbrough was unbelievable but what followed was pretty sensational too. We took on Reading next in the fourth round, another tricky tie as they were a division above us and had some good players like Michael Gilkes and Steve Moran. We were at home but we could only draw 1–1 in the first game. Marc North scored our equaliser but even though we had loads of other chances and Richard O'Kelly hit the woodwork a couple of times, it finished as a draw so it went to a replay. Most people thought our opportunity had gone and we didn't stand much of a chance at their place.

But in the replay we were the better team and were deservedly beating them when Shaun Cunnington put us 1–0 up in the second half. I had to come off with an injury and we started to look a bit rocky with Kevin Jobling having to play as an emergency right-back. Just as we thought we were going to hang on, Moran equalised and it looked like it would go to extra time when we would surely be on the back foot.

However, it never came to those extra 30 minutes because amazingly Gilkes, who had been terrorising for most of the game, played a hopeless back-pass to his own goalkeeper from the halfway line – and Kev, who had been given the run around by Gilkes all night, got the last laugh on him by picking up the loose ball, rounding the keeper and slotting home the winner. It was an incredible turn of events.

Suddenly we were in the fifth round, which was virtually unheard of for a Fourth Division club like Grimsby. When we played Wimbledon for a place in the quarter-finals it was just at the time when there was a huge craze in football for fans to carry inflatables with them to games. Manchester City probably started it with giant inflatable bananas but other clubs joined in – Stoke had pink panthers, West Ham had hammers and Arsenal had fried eggs.

But Grimsby had one of the most famous inflatables of them all – Harry the Haddock. The craze was at its height for our trip to Wimbledon, which really added to the atmosphere. The draw was a bit of a disappointment in some ways because their ground Plough Lane was a bit of a dump and not really the kind of place you would associate with a glamorous top flight club. But Wimbledon were an established First Division club at that time even though they had been a non-league team not too many years earlier – and more than that they were the holders, having famously beaten Liverpool at Wembley the previous year.

I had hurt my ankle ligaments at Reading so I was out injured for that game. Instead of travelling down to the game with the rest of the team, I went down as a fan with a couple of mates. Before the game we went round a few pubs and everywhere you went you could see these Harry the Haddocks being waved around. It was like an invasion and must have given everyone playing a great lift when they saw the support they were getting from the Mariners fans.

When I got to Plough Lane I was amazed to find the ground staff watering the pitch – not just watering it but absolutely flooding it with hosepipes, presumably to make it as heavy and muddy as possible. Grimsby might have been three divisions below Wimbledon but they knew we were a proper footballing side who liked to get it down and pass it around so they were trying to scupper our style of play. I think they knew if it came down to a straight game of football we might batter them. They had some big-name players, though, people like John Fashanu, Terry Phelan, Dennis Wise and Vinnie Jones – although Vinnie was suspended for the FA Cup tie against us.

I went behind the goal and when big Keith Alexander headed us in front in the first half from a John Cockerill corner it was a fantastic feeling. There was actually a photo in one of the newspapers of that goal with thousands of these haddocks being waved where you can see me in my suede jacket cheering my head off. But Wimbledon came back into it and scored twice in quick succession in the second half to go 2–1 up. First Fashanu bundled one over the line where it might easily have been given as a foul on our keeper Steve Sherwood and then Wise scored as well.

Marc North was pushed further forward to try to get an equaliser and twice he nearly did too. He was through on goal but was given offside both times, the second time he put it in the net right at the end and we thought for a moment he had made it 2–2 until we saw the linesman's flag. They then broke away up to the other end and made it 3–1 to finish the game off but we took them to the wire, we really did, and I'm convinced that if we had got a draw we would have beaten them in a replay.

# 7

# Up The Football League We Go

The FA Cup run of 1988/89 gave us all great memories but finishing ninth in the league wasn't good enough for Alan Buckley. Right from the very start, he was always looking to improve the squad.

Towards the end of that first season he had brought in a player called Dave Gilbert who was similar in style to Gary Childs but played on the opposite flank. He also signed Tony Rees, who I think was one of the best centre-forwards Grimsby Town ever had in my time at the club. He had started out as a youngster with Aston Villa where he had won the FA Youth Cup, then he had done well at Birmingham City and he was also a full Welsh international.

In many ways, Tony was more of a playmaker than a traditional centre-forward and he wasn't a particularly prolific goalscorer but with those two in the side, Alan really started to get us playing. Tony also had an incredibly strong pair of legs – they made Mark Hughes look like a weakling. That meant you could bang the ball hard in towards him and play off him.

When Buckley signed Garry Birtles and Paul Futcher, who both had a fantastic amount of experience, you could tell he meant business. With Garry, it really brought it home to the rest of us just how much this guy had achieved when he brought his European Cup winner's medal in one day. It was tiny, just like a little gold coin. It looked like a two pence piece – I was quite disappointed, especially as I like a nice big trophy, as you know! But it did just emphasise his calibre as a player. Here was someone who had won the European Cup – twice in fact – with Nottingham Forest. Garry was coming to the back end of his career but he could still really play.

He was also a diamond fella, a quiet sort but he could be very funny and he also had a tough side to him. He came with a reputation that he could handle himself if it ever came to a fight so no one ever caused any trouble around him.

Garry was a striker but he was so good at that level that he could pretty much play anywhere and sometimes he got dropped back to play alongside Futch. For the rest of us in defence it was an absolute nightmare when that happened. Those two just used to take the piss out of everyone else by playing proper football. Any other centre-half would be trying to boot it forty yards away from danger when they were under pressure or they would head it away. But Gaz and Futch would refuse to do anything like that.

They would be in their own six yard box chesting it and heading it to each other over the head of the other team's centre-forward. I would be yelling at them, 'What are you doing?' and the manager would be on the sidelines having a stroke shouting, 'Clear it!' But they just loved it – they would be trying to nutmeg opponents, which you just didn't do in the Fourth Division.

Playing alongside Futch was quite an experience because his style of play always kept you on tenterhooks. He was the only centre-half I have ever known who wouldn't just head it straight to you, he would glance it to you or he would chest it or side-foot it to you. You never knew what he was going to do next.

It is not what people expect in the Fourth Division and lots of people said you couldn't get out of that league by playing football. But we proved you could. We got it down and passed it and in Alan Buckley's second season we did win promotion in style.

I remember Garry Birtles scoring a hat-trick in our last home game of that season. It was the end of April 1990 and we won 5–1 against Wrexham, who had Joey Jones playing for them – he was another footballing legend who had won the European Cup with Liverpool. He was right at the end of his career but unfortunately he broke his leg in that game and that was pretty much the last we saw of him as a player. It was a shame about Joey but it was a really memorable game for us because it was great to sign off in front of the home fans in such style with one of our biggest wins of the season.

We were under no illusions about the 1990/91 season back in the Third Division. Instead of the likes of Maidstone United and Scarborough, we would be up against much bigger clubs, sides like Bolton Wanderers, Bradford City, Huddersfield Town, Birmingham City, Stoke City and Reading.

When we played Preston North End away early in the season, they had an artificial pitch at Deepdale, which was a completely new experience for me. Our staff did their best to try to get us to wear the right kind of footwear but it was a really unfair advantage for the home team. As we were warming up, we could see they had all kinds of specialist boots on that were designed for the surface whereas some of us were pretty much just wearing Sambas or even ordinary trainers.

Looking back it's amazing to think they were allowed to do it. Preston weren't the only club who experimented with it, there were two or three others as well, but we just didn't have anything like the right sort of preparation. We had a session on the Friday night on AstroTurf but it was only a five-a-side pitch so we were really unprepared.

But Alan just said to us in his team talk, 'Look lads, you've just been promoted and you've done really well. In the new league you're not expected to do anything so just go out and enjoy this league this season. You've earned the right to be here so just go out and enjoy it.'

And with that carefree attitude we went out and amazingly played Preston off the park on their own plastic pitch. To us, although we were under-prepared, we soon realised that what we needed to do was play five-a-side but on a bigger scale – and we had some great five-a-side players, people like Gary Childs, Dave Gilbert and Neil Woods, who was a striker Buckley had brought in that summer and went on to have a big impact.

We beat Preston 3–1 that day and won it at a canter to be honest. From that day on we just seemed to relax and enjoy being in the Third Division. Our feeling was that it was actually an easier league than the one we had just been promoted from. You got more time on the ball, the pitches were better, the crowds were bigger – happy days! We genuinely all found it easier to play in that league so not surprisingly we quickly built up momentum and found ourselves challenging for promotion again.

Everything came down to the last game of the season on 11 May 1991 at home to Exeter City. We needed to win to make sure of going up because Bolton had a much better goal difference than us.

There was a fantastic crowd at Blundell Park, getting on for 15,000, and I felt a bit nervous to be honest because we were all aware of what a big game it was. It was before my time but a lot of older fans still remembered the game against Exeter in 1972 when Grimsby were promoted from the Fourth Division under Lawrie McMenemy. Nineteen years later, Exeter had nothing to play for but they didn't just roll over – in fact, far from it. They had Terry Cooper, the former Leeds and England player, as their manager and his son Mark was playing for them as well.

John Cockerill scored twice for us that day – the first one was from a Paul Futcher free kick which calmed everyone's nerves a bit. Cockers then scored another one just before half-time which should have seen us home and dry, even though looking back it was probably a foul. I just remember him smashing into one of their players from behind and he hit him so hard it forced the ball over the line.

At that point the celebrations had already pretty much started in the Pontoon and we also had Tony Rees back in the team after injury so everything looked rosy. But Mark Cooper scored for Exeter in the second half and Bolton were winning so there were a few palpitations before the final whistle went with us still hanging on to our 2-1 lead. There was a lot of tension in the air and the added time was nerve-racking. An Exeter player called Murray Jones, who later signed for Grimsby, had a shot that was heading agonisingly towards the goal. It felt like it was in slow motion but it hit the post and rebounded to safety.

I have really fond memories of that team. It was a big achievement to go up twice in a row like that – and we did it with the bulk of the players staying the same over the two seasons. The great thing about that era was that we had lads who stayed for years at Grimsby. Once the team had gelled, Alan didn't really tinker with it too much. He brought in someone new if he had to, when someone left.

For example, Andy Tillson was signed by Don Howe at Queens Park Rangers and the manager replaced him with Paul Futcher, a similar player but someone who was already an old head. Futch had been around a bit with clubs like Luton, Manchester City, Oldham and Barnsley and because of his age he was probably only intended as a short-term replacement to start with. But he was such a good player and was so fit that he kept playing with us for a good few years.

It was a great craic that season – partly because we had some real nutcases in that team. There were characters like Paul Reece, a goalkeeper who was a great shot-stopper even though he was really quite small for a keeper; Chris Hargreaves, Kevin Jobling and Mark Lever, who was one of the funniest lads I have ever met, a real clown. They were all lovely lads but they were also nutcases in lots of ways. When those four lads were in the showers together, no one else would dare go in there – you just had no idea what they might do to you. They would be jumping on your back naked, grabbing you, splashing cold water all over you. The rest of us just left them to it – and those four could be in there for an hour together, singing and fighting each other.

It was the same if you walked into the dressing room and those four were in there – you just turned round and walked straight back out again if you had any sense because you knew they would be up to something. They were the four funniest lads going, they really were, and that's partly what made it such a great craic playing for that team.

Another thing that Alan Buckley had done really well was bring in players who were hungry. A lot of them had been down in non-league and were fed up with that, they wanted success. Now that I'm in management myself, I try to use the same way of thinking – I would always choose a player who is hungry over a slightly better player who has just come along for the payday.

Alan knew exactly what he was getting and from that point on, every player he brought into the club fitted into the same mould of what he already had. He would bring in a replacement left-back or a replacement winger of the same type so that they could slot straight into the team without affecting how we played. Later on when Childsy left he signed Kev Donovan, who was exactly the same kind of player who could fit in immediately and didn't disrupt anything. We kept the same style and the same pattern of play with slightly different players.

# 8

# Boiled Eggs And
# Peach Schnapps

Amazingly, the three teams who got promoted in 1990/91 had also all come up from the Fourth Division together – it was Grimsby, Southend United and Cambridge United, not exactly the most glamorous three clubs either.

We had come second the previous season with Southend third and Cambridge winning the play-offs. Exeter, who had been champions, finished in the bottom half in the Third Division the following season but the rest of us all went up again – this time Cambridge were champions, Southend were runners-up and we finished third to get the last automatic promotion spot. Getting back-to-back promotions is quite a feat for any club but for three clubs all to do it simultaneously is quite incredible. I can't imagine it has ever happened before or since in the Football League.

As a reward for getting promoted, the club took us all to Tenerife, which the lads thought was fantastic. I had never been there before but the whole thing was just a blur. I can remember the plane landing there but I can barely remember anything else apart from getting back home again because we were pretty much drunk the whole time. The nightclubs there were open until seven in the morning, we couldn't believe it! We would get back to the hotel, have a boiled egg for breakfast and then go back on the drink almost straight away.

It was bliss but we did get into some scrapes. One day I was in a room with the four likely lads – Paul Reece, Chris Hargreaves, Kev Jobling and Mark Lever – plus a couple of others. In a situation like that you always felt uncomfortable because you just knew something daft was going to happen. Paul Reece had got hold of an aerosol can and because a few of the lads liked an occasional smoke he had also got a lighter and before you knew it he had turned these two into a makeshift flamethrower. He was running round the room with a six or seven inch flame firing it at all the other lads in there. We were all falling over each other trying to get out of the way because we thought we were going to get burnt.

One of the lads tried to escape and ended up trapped on the balcony – four floors up! Luckily his aerosol can ran out before he could do any damage. You really never did know what kind of crazy stuff they would get up to next, those four.

The players loved Tenerife so much that we went back again the following year and this time there were a couple of new additions including Jim Dobbin, a Scottish lad we had brought in from Barnsley. He was a tremendous player, a midfielder who could put it on a sixpence when it came to passing the ball. There was a real togetherness about that squad – it wasn't as if just six or seven of the lads went along to Tenerife, it was all of us, the whole squad. If you tried to do the same thing these days I think you would get about ten players who would just say their wives wouldn't let them go. Alan Buckley pretty much made everyone go, even though he didn't really like to drink. He came with us the first year but he didn't the second time – probably because he realised what we were getting up to.

On the second trip we spent a lot of time in Lineker's Bar, which was the place set up in Tenerife by Gary Lineker's brother and which had become quite a famous bar, especially since the 1990 World Cup in Italy when lots of English football fans descended on there. One time we were outside when all of a sudden a barrage of boiled eggs started flying down at us. We were being pounded by them but at first we couldn't see where they were coming from; a nearby flat or somewhere, we assumed. Some of them weren't even boiled, they were smashing everywhere. Before you knew it, the nutty four lads thought they had spotted where they were coming from, shot off and found themselves barging into a flat full of Spaniards. At this point, I was thinking to myself, 'Hang on, lads, we're going to get ourselves killed here.'

We survived that but also had a few encounters with some lads from the Inter City Firm, who were the notorious West Ham supporters. They were a bit of a dodgy crew but some of them used to work at Lineker's and when they found out we were footballers we somehow got stuck with them during the day when it was pretty much empty. We were chatting to them one day when one of them with a big scar on his face suddenly said, 'Right, get out the back!' I thought, 'Oh no, here we go.'

He got the barman to pick out a big bottle of peach schnapps from behind the bar and took us all round the back where they had table football set up. He put a half-pint glass at one end and another half-pinter at the other end and filled them both up with this peach schnapps. Then he explained the rules of the contest. It was him and one of his ICF mates against two of us Grimsby lads and whenever someone scored a goal the other team had to down their schnapps in one – and it was loser stays on.

Unfortunately my partner was Mark Lever and as anyone in Grimsby knows, he can drink anyone under the table if he puts his mind to it. I am not kidding you, he thought this game was the best thing since sliced bread because it was free booze. He was scoring own goals for fun just so he could get some more down his neck.

'Sorry, Macca!' he would say with a wink and after about six of these things I was sliding down the walls. I really was feeling ill but he just loved it. After that, those West Ham lads seemed to think we were all right and I don't think any of us had to pay for a drink in there again all week. We didn't get many trips away but that was a memorable one.

After those back-to-back promotions we found ourselves in the second tier of English football. We had a really good stint of six seasons in that league, which changed its name during that period from the old Second Division to the new First Division when the Premier League was formed in 1992. We didn't necessarily finish that high up the table but we carried on playing good football under Buckley. We would often outplay decent sides.

Crewe were in the same division as us for part of that time. They were a good team, quite similar to us in lots of ways. They were a small club who were known for being a good footballing side. In fact, some would say they were the best footballing side in that division. But they weren't. They were second behind us. Dario Gradi, who was their manager for years and years, probably wouldn't like to admit it even now but we were a better footballing side than them. They had brought on some really top players who went on to become almost household names, people like Danny Murphy, Craig Hignett and Rob Jones, but whenever we played them we were always the better side. They were close games but we would always out-football them, even at their ground Gresty Road.

Alan had a bit of a ding-dong with Dario in the tunnel on one occasion. Crewe were beating us 1–0 and there was a bit of banter flying around between the two benches. I was injured and I can remember Alan saying to Dario, 'How many goals have you scored in your career? Not 183 like me, eh?'

Dario had no answer to that but just responded by saying, 'Yes, but who's winning at the moment?'

Alan said, 'I can't argue with that. You're beating me at the moment, fair play. I can't give you any stick at the moment.'

That was that for the time being but all the rest of us knew that Alan would be seething deep down so we were all praying for us to score soon. And as soon as we did equalise he couldn't wait to rub it in with the Crewe lads. Straight away he was telling Dario in no uncertain terms that he had never kicked a ball in his life. Alan loved getting one back over him.

In some ways there was quite a fierce rivalry between Grimsby and Crewe because we were both small clubs trying to do similar things in a league where we were up against some much bigger clubs. I think we were also upset because Crewe used to get all the plaudits for their style of play whereas poor old Grimsby didn't because we weren't a fashionable club.

We had some great cup runs under Alan, too. Grimsby have had quite a reputation for being a good team in the League Cup which seemed to go back to when Dave Booth was manager and before I had even signed a YTS. In 1984/85 Grimsby had knocked out Everton and got through to the quarter-finals before losing to Norwich City. Blundell Park was a real fortress in cup matches – it was often freezing cold, with a fierce wind blowing in off the sea, the fans were close to the pitch and big teams just didn't seem to fancy it. There was a phenomenal atmosphere, especially for night matches and we rarely seemed to lose cup ties at home.

Early in the 1991/92 season we played Aston Villa over two legs in the League Cup and managed to beat them on the away goals rule. That was a big draw for us at the time because Ron Atkinson was their manager and they had some really high-profile players like Dwight Yorke, Cyrille Regis, Steve Staunton, Paul McGrath and Gordon Cowans.

We drew 0–0 in the first leg at Blundell Park in front of another big crowd of nearly 14,000 and for the return match at Villa Park it was tin hats for us for nearly the whole 90 minutes. Shaun Teale got a goal for Villa but Dave Gilbert scored a penalty for us and we managed to hang on to go through on away goals. The nearest Villa came to getting a winner was when Dwight Yorke burst through and only had our goalkeeper Steve Sherwood to beat. I just managed to catch up with him and as I tackled him my foot went over the top of the ball and I somehow managed to drag it back away from him. He went flying and Ron Atkinson was screaming his head off for a penalty – in fact every Villa supporter in the ground was.

I thought to myself, 'If the ref gives a penalty now and we get knocked out, I'll be gutted because it wasn't a foul.'

But he didn't give it – rightly so – and as I got up off the ground it was a brilliant feeling. I had a little swagger because I felt like a top player, as if I was the sort of defender who made perfectly-timed goal-saving tackles like that all the time.

The other unusual thing about that tie was Mark Lever being sick on Cyrille Regis's back. Big 'Un used to get really nervous and pretty much every week he would throw up with nerves – sometimes even at half-time. He would go in the dressing room, have several glasses of orange juice and then throw up. No wonder he was sick! On the pitch against Villa, I could hear him retching while we were playing and before I knew it, he had been sick all over Regis's shoulder and back. Poor Big 'Un was trying to wipe it off with his shirt and saying, 'Sorry, Cyrille!' Cyrille wasn't best pleased, to say the least!

Tottenham Hotspur beat us in the next round but the following season we had another cracking tie over two legs in the League Cup, this time against QPR. They were riding high in the Premier League at the time and had Les Ferdinand banging in goals left, right and centre. We only lost 2–1 at their place and beat them by the same scoreline back at Blundell Park but got knocked out on penalties.

When Grimsby first started getting success, it was inevitable that other bigger clubs would be interested in Alan Buckley. Leicester City wanted him at one stage but he turned them down and eventually he got another offer, this time from West Bromwich Albion, an offer he felt he couldn't refuse. He left for The Hawthorns in 1994 and everyone at Blundell Park was sad to see him go. Unfortunately, he took quite a few of our players to West Brom with him – first Tony Rees, then Dave Gilbert, Paul Agnew and Chris Hargreaves. Later he also signed Paul Groves and Paul Crichton. By the time he had finished he had more or less taken the entire left hand side of the team with him.

I think his idea was to take one half of the Grimsby team with him and then gradually get the other side of the team to gel together as well. But it never really worked out for Alan at West Brom – he was only there for about two and a half years before getting the sack because he hadn't got the team up to where the club wanted them to be, challenging for promotion.

West Brom were in the same league as us at the time but it was understandable that he would want to move there because they were a much bigger club than Grimsby and had much more potential. We clashed with them a few times while he was in charge there. That was interesting for me, to see how Buckley worked from the opposition point of view. As well as all the lads he took to The Hawthorns with him from Grimsby, he had some other good players, people like big Bob Taylor, But Alan couldn't get them to play like he wanted them to play.

They did OK but I don't think the players who were already there really understood what he was trying to do and the West Brom old guard didn't take to such a large number of Grimsby players coming in. The Baggies' supporters also regarded themselves as a big club so they felt they should be getting big-name players in – not people from the likes of Grimsby. To be honest, it wasn't far removed from our attitude at first when Buckley came to Grimsby and started bringing in non-league players. But on that occasion he was given time to make it work and in the end it paid off.

Once Alan had gone, there was a lot of interest in the manager's job at Grimsby. And when Brian Laws came in with Kenny Swain as his assistant, the reaction was very positive. Brian was quite young for a manager and was going to continue playing, which was quite exciting for us because we knew he was a good player with real pedigree, having been at Middlesbrough and Nottingham Forest. Kenny was another one who had a European Cup medal, like Garry Birtles. He had won his with Aston Villa. In many ways, Brian fitted in quite well with what we had been used to because he had started to learn the ropes under Brian Clough and Alan Buckley had started his career at Nottingham Forest and had also been brought up trying to play football in the Clough style. In some ways Alan thought he was the new Brian Clough.

So when Brian Laws came to Blundell Park, nothing changed drastically. We carried on playing in quite a similar style, maybe a little bit more direct, trying to get the ball into the box slightly quicker but that was all. Lawsy still quite fancied himself as a player even though he was well into his 30s by this stage and he did play quite a bit for us while he was manager. Some people got the idea that he took my place in the team at right-back but that's not true. He never took my place but he generally played there if I was injured. If I was fit, I would play. I always got on well with Lawsy and I also liked Kenny.

Kenny was one of those people who would give you confidence. If you went up to him before a match and told him you were worried about a winger you were coming up against, he would really give you a boost and nine times out of ten you would end up playing really well just because of the lift he had given you. Kenny was another right-back so he really helped me a lot. He had been a brilliant player and could hit the ball just as sweetly with his left as he could with his right.

He absolutely loved coaching and we used to nickname him 'Kenny Cones' because he would seemingly always walk around with dozens of cones under his arms eager to put them out at a moment's notice for little coaching sessions. With some lads, all they really wanted to do in training was play games of five-a-side but Kenny was mad about actual coaching. He would put so many discs and cones out that the training ground looked like a runway where an aeroplane was about to land.

Having a player-manager definitely felt different to how it had been like before. During training, if we were having a game and Brian was having a stinker, some of the senior players wouldn't be able to resist giving him a bit of stick. I would be thinking to myself, 'Be careful, lads, this is the manager of the club you're talking to – you can't speak to him like that!' But they didn't care, they would be saying, 'Kenny! Take the manager off, he's rubbish!'

It was all quite a contrast to the dictator style of management which we had been used to under previous managers, particularly Mick Lyons. With Brian, he would have a laugh with you, he was a bit more one of the lads.

One of the new players we signed at that time was Tony Gallimore, who soon told us he had a bit of a reputation as someone who liked the booze. We had gone out one afternoon and he told us when he was at Carlisle United they had called him Tony Gallon-more and his other nickname was 'Distillery'. He boasted, 'I could drink any of you lot under the table.'

Big words. The only thing was, we started drinking at lunchtime and by half past five in the afternoon he was slumped on the table. We were thinking to ourselves, 'So much for the distillery guy!' We were laughing at him but to be fair to him, he had drunk plenty in those five hours and we soon found out that it was true that he could put it away.

Not long after Gally arrived, we went to Jersey on a team trip. Kenny was giving out envelopes with details of who you would be sharing a room with and I was complaining, 'I bet you a tenner I end up with that Tony Gallimore. That would be just my luck.' I turned round and there he was, standing there, listening! I was mortified because I would never back-stab anyone but that's what it must have sounded like. All I meant was that I might end up getting into trouble if I was sharing with him and he lived up to his boozy reputation.

'Don't you want to share with me then?' he was saying. I couldn't apologise enough. I told him, 'Don't worry, it's nothing to do with you. It's just that I always seem to get put in with the new lads and it's sometimes hard work sharing with someone you've only just met.'

So I did end up sharing with Gally and it turned out to be a real stroke of luck because he is one of the nicest lads I have ever come across in football – and he is on a par with Mark Lever as being one of the funniest. We stayed room-mates after that all the time we were playing together and we never had a cross word between us.

He used to have me crying with laughter sometimes. Gally was leathered quite a lot of the time, that much is true, but we had a memorable time together. He used to do a wicked Mick Jagger impression, cocking his hand and sticking his chest out and singing some of the famous Rolling Stones songs. It was brilliant.

As part of this trip to Jersey we were booked to play a round of golf at quite a posh links course. Everyone was supposed to take their own bag of clubs but I wasn't really a golfer and didn't have any so I borrowed some from the physio John Fraser. I can't hit a golf ball to save my life and neither can Gally to be honest. Somehow we ended up in a four together with Ian Knight, who was the youth team guy, and Mark Lever, who could play a bit – or so he thought.

As soon as we turned up we knew we were in trouble because the greenkeeper marched up to us and said, 'What the hell are those on your feet?' We were wearing ordinary trainers because that's all we had but he said we had to wear proper golf shoes.

'OK, where do we hire them from?' I said. 'Hire them? What are you talking about? You have to buy them!'

Sixty quid it cost me to buy these white golf shoes before we could even start playing – and it didn't get any better when we finally got onto the first tee.

The greenkeeper was still there keeping an eye on us. We were the last group to go out and he obviously sensed trouble because he was saying things like, 'I hope you're going to take it seriously, lads. We take your sport seriously.'

We might have been the last to go out but we were clearly the worst four in all of our party. Mark went first – at least he looked the part, he had all the right gear – and his first shot he managed to ping straight about 100 yards. Then Knighty went next. I have no idea what he thought he looked like because he had sunglasses on but he was also wearing a bobble hat – and the shades were so big they looked like some sort of ski mask. He had some sort of spats on as well – he looked a disgrace, he really did. He took a big swing – and the ball didn't move. We all fell about laughing but Knighty insisted it was just a practice swing. Then he had another 'practice swing' and his third effort just about connected with the top of the ball enough to knock it off the tee – yet he insisted that was yet another practice shot!

By this time the greenkeeper had gone from being quite good-humoured with us to being a bit more serious and finally to being properly angry. When Knighty eventually did manage a proper shot all he managed to do was whack it straight into the sea – but Gally did even worse. He chose the biggest club he could find, took a huge swipe and hit it quite hard. But unfortunately it veered off course, hit the tractor that the greenkeeper had been sitting on and flew straight back behind us. He had sent it 150 yards but in totally the wrong direction!

I was panicking about what on earth would happen to my shot but by this time the greenkeeper had stormed off in a fury, swearing to himself. My tee shot went into the sea as well but after that we relaxed and just had a laugh among ourselves as we went round the course. I think we got as far as the ninth hole but we were truly terrible. Gally was chipping it off the greens, that's how bad he was, and I had got massive blisters from my new shoes. My feet were cut to ribbons.

Halfway round, the greenkeeper turned up again, stomped up to us and said: 'You, you, you and you – off!' He had actually been to see whoever was in charge of the whole course and got us thrown off before we could finish our round. I was delighted because my feet were in tatters – and I sold the shoes to someone else on the tenth hole for £20. As you can imagine, I have never been a massive fan of golf since that day.

It was a great trip overall and the manager joined in with a lot of the fun. We found him out one night, though, when we were playing cards. Lawsy never seemed to lose – he always seemed to keep pulling out a King when he needed one. So some of the lads stitched him up by sharing out the four Kings in the pack and then next time he pulled out a King, we said: 'A King – that's strange because I've got a King, he's got a King, he's got a King and he's also got a King!' That was five Kings – so we made him go in the middle and drink a pint down in one for trying to pull a fast one.

On another occasion during that trip, a few of us were in one of the hotel rooms with the manager when there was a knock on the door. We all went outside into the corridor and Lawsy was wearing just a towel wrapped round him because he had just had a shower. As we got outside the room, the door slammed shut behind us. And as soon as that happened,

Steve Livingstone just looked him up and down and said: 'You know what's going to happen now, don't you?'

Here we were, three floors up in a hotel, with the manager of the football club separated from his clothes. Lawsy immediately twigged he was going to try to grab his towel from him and leave him totally naked so before you knew it, he was off legging it to safety. Livvo was chasing him up and down the corridors – he was desperate to get that towel off him so he would be forced to go down to reception stark naked and ask for a spare key. This was a player chasing his own manager!

I don't think it would happen in any other club. You certainly wouldn't get away with that sort of thing these days. No one caught him so he got away with it with his modesty intact. Actually, Brian Laws was very quick when he wanted to be – he was like Ben Johnson.

While we were in Jersey, Lawsy was cleverly trying to negotiate contracts with people. He knew he had people tied down for the duration of the trip so it was a good time for him to do it. That meant a lot of the players were avoiding him because we would rather be doing contracts back at the club when you could properly see what all the options were and didn't feel your hand was being forced. But I agreed to meet him while we were there to discuss a new contract, which was quite an important one for me because I was due to have a testimonial as I had now been at the club for ten years.

What he told me was if I signed the new deal that was on offer he would get Nottingham Forest to play in my testimonial. That sounded like a really attractive proposition because Forest were a really good side at that time. Players like Stan Collymore, Brian Roy and Steve Stone had really transformed them into a top side and they had qualified for

Europe. It was in that period when English clubs were just being allowed back into Europe after being banned because of Heysel so there was a lot of excitement around the UEFA Cup. So I thought that sounded like it would be a brilliant testimonial, we would get a full house and the place would be buzzing. I was happy to sign a new deal but in the end the Forest idea fell through and we got Leeds United instead.

When people first started talking about commemorating my ten years at the club, the idea was to do a whole testimonial year. I was told it would be tax-free, which suited me down to the ground, but you had to get a proper committee with a secretary and treasurer and so on. I decided I definitely wanted the physio John Fraser involved and we also recruited an ex-player called Dave Boylen, who was a Mariners legend in his own right. He had played nearly 400 times for Grimsby in the 1960s and 1970s and was part of Lawrie McMenemy's team who won the Fourth Division title in 1972 – but more importantly for our committee, he knew absolutely everyone. If we ever needed any contacts for any of the events we were organising or if we ever needed to sell tickets for anything, Dave was the man. He could put bums on seats and I felt it would be nice to keep a connection with the club from an earlier era.

We got a guy called Barry Meadows to be chairman of the committee and another ex-Mariner called Jim Lumby was also involved. Barry was a great person to have on board because he seemed to know so many useful people in Cleethorpes and Grimsby and Jim ran a pub called the Hainton and had great contacts with the Bass brewery so he got them to sponsor some of our events. We also had fantastic help from Jenny Collishaw who was secretary of the committee.

The same people also went on to run a charity called the Artie White Foundation which was started during my testimonial year. Artie was an ex-footballer who died of a heart attack and the foundation was set up to raise money for good causes in his memory. It has raised hundreds of thousands of pounds over the years.

So you can see we had a great committee for my testimonial year and right from the start the whole thing was brilliant, starting with a big family fun day at Littlefield Lane. One of the highlights was a dinner with George Best and Rodney Marsh as the after-dinner speakers, which was amazing. I was supposed to pick them up in a taxi with the club's commercial manager Tony Richardson and when I arrived, there they were having fish and chips. Two absolute legends of football tucking into fish and chips in the Blundell Hotel! I was almost frozen with awe.

When we got introduced, George said to me, 'Hope you don't mind John but we go to a lot of these events where it's always the same – chicken or steak, soup, melon. If I'm coming to Grimsby I want fish and chips. And not in a restaurant where they only give you the tail end, I want proper fish shop stuff.'

I ended up in the back of the taxi with George on the way to the Winter Gardens where the event was being held. I was still pinching myself that this was me with one of the greatest footballers that had ever lived – and yet he was asking me questions all about myself. It didn't seem right – it felt like it should have been the other way round.

George was a lovely guy but when he started to have a couple of drinks, Rodney rolled his eyes – he must have seen it all before. When we sat at the table, George helped himself to a bottle of red and a bottle of white and kept them by his feet. At that point Rodney nudged me to say that I had better ask the committee to get George on to do his bit as soon as possible.

George was a gent but he did want his fee paying in cash and at one point he was saying he wasn't going to sign some autographs. That was where Dave Boylen came in handy. He made it clear he wouldn't get paid a penny if he didn't sign the autographs. You don't argue with Dave and sure enough the autographs got signed  and George got paid by cheque as well.

The testimonial game itself was in August 1996 against Leeds, who had a good side and were still managed by Howard Wilkinson, who had won the league with them not many seasons before. They had people like Ian Rush, Gary Kelly and Brian Deane playing for them and also a very young Harry Kewell. There had been rumours that Leeds were interested in signing me at one point but Howard apparently thought I was a couple of inches too short and in any case they had a young Irish kid coming through who turned out to be Gary Kelly. He played in my testimonial too – but he is barely any taller than me, mind you!

The game had been arranged as the final pre-season fixture just a week before the league programme was due to start which was a really nice gesture by the chairman Bill Carr. The club could easily have said that it was right in the middle of pre-season and they needed a more serious warm-up.

But on the morning of the game it was pouring down. I thought, 'Typical! Of all the days. Now no one's going to turn out to watch if it's like this.' Fortunately at about eleven o'clock in the morning the sun came out and it was red hot so it turned out that we got a really decent crowd and it was a fantastic day. I was so grateful to Bill for what he did for me that day – and it wasn't just Bill. We didn't get charged anything for all the stewards and staff who worked on the day, not to mention the police.

We had some caricatures done which we gave to all the players taking part, although I think some of them looked nothing like who they were supposed to be. We also got some bottles of wine to give to the Leeds lads afterwards. I have no idea where on earth they came from – they weren't the best quality, that's for sure. They had Grimsby Town labels stuck on them but it was probably Pomagne or something underneath. I remember Rushy taking one look at a bottle and muttering, 'I put this sort of stuff on my chips.'

# 9

# It's Only A Scratch

Working with someone like Brian Laws was a real insight into a different style of management. The Jersey trip showed he was much more like one of the lads, mainly because he was also still a player himself. That can be an advantage for getting your ideas across – but it didn't save him from getting sacked when the team began to struggle.

We got off to a bad start in the 1996/97 season and he paid the price by losing his job that November. But the writing had been on the wall for Brian after what became known as the notorious 'plate of chicken' incident the previous season.

At the centre of it all was a player we had signed called Ivano Bonetti in 1995, an Italian who had played for big clubs like Juventus and won the Serie A title. Ivano was a big hit with the fans right from the start but there were various complications to do with an American management company that he was contracted to. Because this company owned various rights, it was going to cost £100,000 for him to stay at Blundell Park. And unfortunately there was a FIFA rule that meant Grimsby weren't allowed to deal directly with the company – not that they could have afforded that sort of money anyway.

But Ivano was so popular at the club that the fans ended up raising money towards the fee needed. They were doing bucket collections, going round pubs and doing fundraising events, it was a magnificent effort and they did raise half the cash – Ivano then stumped up the rest of the money himself. A lot of people said it was very similar to what had happened years previously when the Grimsby fans got together to raise money to buy Joe Waters – and he was one of the club's all-time greats so it shows what good company Bonetti was in.

Bonetti was a great player, he really was. He had powerful legs on him and a great left foot. He didn't speak very good English so he would whistle for the ball if he wanted it. Particularly in training you would hear him whistling all the time during a game and if you stopped, even for a split second, he would nip in and take it off you as quick as a flash. Ivano had great ability and when he was on song there was no one else like him.

We played West Brom quite soon after he had joined us and were drawing 0–0. He scored the winner for us and as soon as it had gone into the back of the net, he was off. He ran right round the back of the goal, all along the whole length of the stand where our supporters were, past the West Brom dugout, past our dugout – and all the while he was clapping the outstretched hands of the Grimsby fans.

Of course, it was a very special win for our fans because West Brom were managed by Alan Buckley and had quite a few of our ex-players – and Ivano certainly recognised the importance of the occasion. He must have clapped the hand of every single one of our fans who were in there. And from that moment on, he became an instant cult figure at Blundell Park.

The very next week there were Ivano Bonetti flags everywhere at the ground – not just small flags but giant Italian ones with his face on them. People were wearing T-shirts as well – the whole place was like one big Ivano Bonetti fan club and to be honest it was a great feeling to be part of it all.

It wasn't just the supporters that he was popular with – he was the most generous bloke I have ever met so the rest of the players loved him as well. He was seemingly very well off and was always buying you drinks or treating people to pizzas if you went out for a meal.

Out of all the players, Ivano particularly befriended me, Paul Groves and a lad called Craig Shakespeare who had joined us from West Brom a couple of years earlier – we all got on really well together.

One week in February 1996 we had a couple of games down south in the space of a few days – West Ham away first of all in a midweek FA Cup match and then Luton away the following Saturday in the league – so it was decided that we would stay over down south rather than travel back up to Grimsby in between.

Ivano had invited me, Grovesy and Shakey over to his place in Italy for the weekend – a beautiful spot near Lake Garda. Even though we had drawn with West Ham in the cup game, which meant a replay a week later, Brian Laws had cleared it for us to fly to Italy on the Saturday evening and stay there on the Sunday as long as we were back for the Monday. But as luck would have it, a bout of food poisoning spread through the hotel where we were staying after the West Ham game and we all got it. Typical!

Several of us weren't fit for the Luton match on the Saturday, including me. But even as I sat in the stand unable to play with this food poisoning, I was thinking to myself, 'I'm still going away for the weekend – I've never been to Italy before and I'm not going to miss this.' Ivano was paying for the whole trip because he was so generous – none of us were being asked to shell out a penny towards it.

The game against Luton was nip and tuck and towards the end we were hanging on for what would have been a valuable point so Lawsy was shouting out orders for everyone to keep it tight and get the ball in the corners. Ivano wasn't that sort of player though. He was caught in possession fannying about with it in a dangerous area and next thing you knew Luton went up the other end and scored a late winner.

Those of us who had been watching from the stand knew the manager would be absolutely livid. I headed for the dressing room and that was when everything kicked off. I was only really halfway in through the door so I didn't get the clearest view of what was going on but it was obvious that Brian was getting riled watching the players having their post-match food. Brian was saying to the players, 'Is that it? Is that all that you're bothered about? Getting your sandwiches?'

A sandwich got tossed towards Brian and before you knew it, fists were flying and Ivano was on the deck. It all happened so quickly, it was hard to take in what was going on. What was for certain was that Ivano's face was half caved in and there was blood everywhere with Kenny Swain trying to mop it up from the floor with a bib. There was total commotion – here was our best player with blood pouring out of his face.

Ivano's brother was there and became very agitated. He was keen to let everyone know straight away that Ivano had plenty of money and could afford a good lawyer. But I have to confess, all I could think about what was going to happen to my weekend in Italy? We were there with our suitcases all packed. I felt like saying to Ivano, 'Come on man, it's only a scratch – what's up with you?'

The way the story was told in the media, Brian had supposedly thrown a plate of chicken at Ivano – but that was just a newspaper story that made a good headline.

As we bundled our suitcases back on the bus, we were grumbling our heads off but there was nothing to be done about it. Ivano's injuries were actually worse than I first thought – he had to have an operation on his cheekbone and ended up with a scar on his face.

When it came to the cup replay against West Ham a few days later, Ivano was still sore about the whole thing but he had to come on to the pitch beforehand and pretend to everyone that he and Lawsy were still friends. They were shaking hands as if there was no animosity even though Ivano still had a massive black eye.

Somehow all the furore that surrounded that incident must have inspired us because we went out and beat West Ham 3–0 that night and knocked them out of the FA Cup. After the game, Ivano invited some of the lads out for something to eat but it soon became obvious that what he really wanted was for all of us to give statements siding with him and going against the manager. But that seemed very risky and we weren't keen on going down that route.

To rub salt into our wounds, we gradually found out more and more about the amazing weekend in Italy that I had missed out on, along with Grovesy and Shakey. We were supposed to have been driven down to the airport in a limo, then picked up in a limo at the other end and whisked off to a millionaires' party at Lake Garda. I was gutted!

The plan had been for us to have gone out to a nightclub with some of Ivano's best friends, who turned out to be Gianluca Vialli and Gianluca Pagliuca. He had mentioned famous footballers like them before but I had always assumed he was just name-dropping, but not a bit of it. They had all played together at Sampdoria and were best mates. When they won the Italian league title against all the odds and by beating all the big guns, those three were part of the crazy celebrations that followed when they famously all bleached their hair for the last game of the season.

By the time Ivano started telling us how they had been planning to take us to see the Milan derby the next day, I was just telling him, 'Please, no more – don't tell me any more, I don't want to know!' I was mortified.

John Aldridge took him to Tranmere Rovers in the end which was a good thing for everyone. Grimsby wanted rid of him, he wanted to get out and Tranmere got a top quality player so everyone was happy. But I did stay in touch with Ivano and when we were due to play Tranmere not long after he had left, he wrote me a letter saying he was looking forward to seeing me but also asking, 'You won't kick me, will you?' I didn't reply but we both knew that I would be up against him because I would be playing right-back and he would be on their left wing.

When I saw him in the tunnel I leant over to him and just said, 'Sorry I didn't reply to your letter but I'm going to kick the shit out of you. Nothing personal.' Lo and behold, he was substituted supposedly with a pulled hamstring not long into the game – he had fallen for it hook, line and sinker!

Ivano went back to Italy eventually but he did come back to the UK a few years later when he took over as manager of Dundee and brought in some amazing signings, top players like the Argentinian Claudio Caniggia.

I have been in touch with him a few times since but I never did manage to get my visit to his place in Lake Garda. Maybe it was for the best – it might have been a bit embarrassing when Ivano bought a round of drinks. He would have been ordering the most expensive champagne all round and I would have been asking for a bottle of Heineken.

After beating West Ham just after the Ivano Bonetti fracas, we got a great draw in the fifth round of the FA Cup – Chelsea at home. They weren't such a massive club then as they are now but they were still big guns as far as we were concerned. Glenn Hoddle was the manager at the time and they had some top players like Dan Petrescu, Ruud Gullit and Mark Hughes.

It was a freezing cold night and the pitch was solid – in fact it probably shouldn't have been played. Blundell Park was packed to the rafters, with temporary seating specially installed so there were nearly 10,000 there and it was the perfect conditions for a giant-killing.

Terry Phelan was in their side, someone I knew from having played him when he was at Wimbledon. He was a really good player but I always thought he was too nice as a footballer. Early on in the game, I crunched into a fifty-fifty tackle with him and I immediately thought, 'Hello, he doesn't fancy this.' I had the better of him after that and Gary Childs was causing him all sorts of problems.

Maybe they didn't have the right kind of boots on for icy conditions but Chelsea were struggling to stay on their feet while we were dancing round them. They took us too lightly and we should have beaten them that night but it ended up 0–0. I had a great chance to win it right at the end when Neil Woods back-heeled it to me – I hit it first time whereas if I had taken a touch I maybe would have scored. I only scored thirteen goals in my career and I think five or six of those were from exactly the same move, finishing with me drilling it into the far corner. Whenever I have scored I can always visualise it going into the net as soon as I hit it but on this occasion I just dragged it wide.

In the replay at Stamford Bridge, we still played well but Chelsea won 4–1. They just had that bit of extra quality in the final third and Mark Hughes's movement was phenomenal. Dennis Wise said to me during the game, 'You've met a different kettle of fish tonight, haven't you?'

The chairman, Bill Carr, tried to smooth things over as best he could after the Ivano Bonetti incident because I don't think he really liked sacking people but the writing was on the wall for Brian Laws. However, it wasn't until quite a few months later in November 1996 that Lawsy was finally sacked. His assistant Kenny Swain took over as manager for a while, first as caretaker until the end of the season although somehow I never thought he would end up in the job permanently.

As it was, we got relegated on the last game of the season. Even though we beat Southend 4–0, Bradford also won against QPR so we were down. At that point, Kenny told me I should look to move on from Grimsby. He said, 'You should still be playing First Division football, you're in your prime and too good to be going down to the third tier.'

I got on really well with Kenny so I agreed to go with him to a hotel and golf complex near Brigg called Forest Pines to meet a couple of agents who he said could sort me out with a new club.

I had never had an agent before and my first impression of these two was hilarious – they were both Scousers, one was quite heavy and thick-set and the other was really small and skinny. When I shook their hand, all I could hear was a jingling sound as all their gold bracelets and jewellery slipped forward down their sleeve. I thought, 'Here we go, we've got a right pair of scallywags here – I think it's Billy and Icky!'

They were probably perfectly good agents but one of the first things they said to me was, 'Do you play golf?' That put my nose out of joint straight away. I thought we were there to talk about football not golf, which I'm terrible at, as you know. Presumably they were making the point that lots of deals with club chairmen get agreed over a game of golf.

They told me they could get me a move to Tranmere, who had finished mid-table in the First Division and had John Aldridge as their player-manager. But I didn't fancy going there – we seemed to have built up a bit of rivalry with them over the years because we had usually been in the same league as them.

The agents were also talking about the percentage that they would be taking and all I could think was, 'Percentage of what? You haven't got me anything yet.' So I pretty much made up my mind straight away that I didn't want to get involved.

Soon after that meeting, I spoke to another Grimsby player called Clive Mendonca. He suggested I should meet his agent Mel Stein, who was representing Paul Gascoigne at the time. That sounded more like it – and I ended up with Mel for two years in the end. He did well by me during that time and got me a good increase on what I had been earning – the first time I ever got a signing-on fee was also thanks to Mel.

But after two years I felt I had learnt enough and could demand decent money myself without needing an agent any more. Mel opened my eyes to how much people of my age playing at my level were actually getting compared to me. I was never a greedy player and if the money on offer was decent, I would sign. Having said that, there were times as a young player when I went to Alan Buckley's office asking for a pay rise. I would soon be shown the door – sometimes with a tea cup flying past my earhole.

Once I was with Mel, I put in a transfer request, not because I wanted to leave Grimsby but because I did want to play football at the highest level I could achieve for my ability, as Kenny Swain had suggested. Shortly after that, I was heading off to Amsterdam with some friends on what was supposedly a football tournament but what was actually an excuse to go on the lash and just as we were waiting to be picked up by the coach at Grimsby bus depot, someone brought over a copy of that day's *Grimsby Evening Telegraph*.

The back page had a story splashed all over it about me wanting to leave. I wasn't really all that serious about leaving Grimsby and I had no idea it would cause such a stir. I didn't know what sort of reaction I would get if I was spotted by fans so I shoved everyone on the bus and got us to hurry away as fast as possible in the hope that things would die down while I was abroad for a few days.

The reaction from the fans was incredible – I was quite touched actually. When I got back from Amsterdam, I had got loads of letters sent to me asking me not to leave Grimsby. People were even sending me tapes with recordings on them and songs like 'Don't Go'.

The next thing I knew I got a phone call from the *Telegraph* sports editor telling me that Alan Buckley was coming back.

# 10

# Not So Mickey Mouse

The return of Alan Buckley changed things – but it still didn't alter the fact that I felt Kenny was right about me being at a higher level than Grimsby were going to be playing the following season. When I spoke to Alan, he told me he knew about my transfer request and said he could see I had become disheartened.

Alan said, 'All I want from you is to give me a couple of months and let me prove to you that I mean business. If we're not doing well after a couple of months and you can't see that it's happening, then we'll move you on.'

I liked his honesty and I liked the way he played his football, plus we had always got on really well so I signed on for the next season and never really looked to move away from Blundell Park again after that. There were a couple of times when other clubs were interested in me but I certainly never put in a transfer request again.

Under Alan, the team spirit was soon back to how it was in the good old days – although it took a little while for us to start to get a decent run of results.

The atmosphere was great for me in that second spell. Sometimes in Alan's first spell, some of the younger lads like me were a bit intimidated by him because it was quite a regimented style of management but once you got to know him, things seemed a bit more relaxed second time around and we all had confidence that he would bring us success. I felt he would get us to the highest level we were capable of so I wasn't worried about it when we didn't get the results at first that season.

Looking back, 1997/98 was a strange year because at the start of the season you couldn't have imagined where it was going to lead us the following May. Having been relegated and got a new manager, we had a bit of a new-look squad.

Alan Buckley had brought in a few new players like Kevin Donovan and one or two others. Kev was quite an important signing for me because he would be the one I would need to be striking up a partnership with on the right hand side of our team. As a right-back, I had always built up a good relationship with right-wingers in the past.

Kev and I didn't hit it off in the first few games, as players anyway – it wasn't just us two, it was the whole team. We struggled for the first six or seven games of the season. In fact we hadn't won a game in the league and we were right near the bottom of the table.

The manager was scratching his head because he had fancied us to do really well. I wouldn't say we had any emergency team meetings or anything like that but he certainly had a few words to say with us.

And then all of a sudden it just clicked – we went to Fulham and got a really good result. Kev played really well that day and I remember thinking to myself, 'This is it now. I'm really going to enjoy playing with him. I'll be able to get forward with Kev.'

The thing is, I've always been lucky enough to have had decent wingers playing with me, people like Gary Childs and Tommy Watson. These were players who stayed with the club for several years so you could build up an understanding with them. It's not like we were chopping and changing the whole time.

So when Kev arrived, that meant he was filling the boots of these lads. The great thing for me was that despite a dodgy start, we soon hit it off playing together and I quickly knew it was going to be fantastic playing with him.

We didn't realise it at the time but when we travelled to play Chesterfield in December 1997 in what was then called the Auto Windscreens Shield, we were taking the first step on what would become our historic journey to Wembley.

That season we ended up playing Chesterfield five times in quite a short space of time so maybe even then we felt there was something unusual in the air. It was strange – we played them home and away in the FA Cup because we drew at Blundell Park and then beat them at their place in the replay. We had them twice in the league and we drew them in the Auto Windscreens Shield too.

To be honest, for us, turning up at Chesterfield that day was just a gesture. We had already had enough of each other. It was coming up to Christmas and we had played them at home the previous Saturday in the FA Cup, then we had to go to their place on the Tuesday, knowing we also had to go back there the following Tuesday for the FA Cup replay! On top of that, we had already just played them once in the league only a month beforehand.

In any case, it was thought of as just being a 'Mickey Mouse cup'. If we had had a choice we probably wouldn't have even entered it. But you did play in it because you had to – even though it was just going through the motions in the early rounds.

We just thought: 'Let's just get through this without getting injured.' So we played the game and honestly, there was virtually no one there watching. There really was almost no interest in it at all and no atmosphere – it felt like we were playing in front of about fifty people. Looking back, it really was a far cry from where we ended up in that competition. Jack Lester scored and we won 1–0 but we really didn't take it seriously.

When we got to the second round, we drew Hull so that was slightly bigger because obviously it was a derby. But even then it was not really regarded as anything special and although we beat them we weren't that bothered. The idea in those early rounds was just to get through the games unscathed more than anything else.

We beat Scunthorpe next, which was again another good local game and that gave us a tie at home to Blackpool, who were a good side.

Looking back at the Blackpool game, it is amazing how even when we beat them we still didn't think much of that victory either. By this stage we were already into February, getting towards the business end of the season but this competition still wasn't really a big deal for us.

Beforehand, someone said to a few of us who were playing, 'You do realise you're in the semi-finals of this, don't you?'

At the time, I don't really think I even realised the final was played at Wembley so this came as a bit of a shock as you can imagine! Even then we were a bit confused because we thought to start with we were in the semi-finals of the whole tournament – until we were told it was just the semis of the northern region.

So as the penny dropped, it started to dawn on us what this could mean. We were in the semi-finals of the northern region. Win that game and then we would be in the northern final, playing for a place at Wembley.

Wembley. Yes, the place where it's everyone's boyhood dream to play. And that was when it really hit home and we understood the possible significance of the tournament for Grimsby Town, a club who had never been to Wembley in their 108-year history.

After beating Blackpool the last team standing between us and a Wembley final were Burnley. We knew it was going to be tough. They had Andy Payton and some other big star players. They were a big club compared to us and they had a massive following.

It was a two-legged affair and the first game was at Blundell Park. It ended up 1–1 and it was quite tight. Obviously you really want to win your home leg so we all thought we had blown it. We really thought we had come so close but fallen at the last hurdle.

All of a sudden the crowds for this competition had started to get bigger, almost without anyone noticing. When we got to Turf Moor we saw straight away that our fans had absolutely packed the away end. That immediately got us thinking, 'Hello, it's game on.' That gave us a real lift.

It was a decent atmosphere and when Lee Nogan scored to put us in the lead, it started to sink in that we were 45 minutes away from going to Wembley.

I'm not kidding you, from that point onwards we threw our bodies at absolutely everything. It was as if someone had thrown a million quid down in front of the eighteen-yard box. We were blocking everything – nothing was going to get past us.

Then in the second half, the ball dropped to Kev Donovan. Now for some reason, he was just one of those players who was always in the right place at the right time. I can remember the ball coming over to him and when he hit it on the volley it nearly ripped the back of the net off. It was an incredible strike. It felt like that was it, game over – after that goal I can't remember a single thing about the actual match. I don't remember what I did, how many touches I had or anything like that.

But I do remember the fans going ballistic and when we got back into the dressing room, the champagne corks were popping and it was an amazing scene of celebration.

Normally, we would never do anything like taking champagne with us to a game because it would just feel like you were counting your chickens. But the bubbly was there – the chairman Bill Carr had brought it with him. We had all really wanted to do it for him as well because he was a great guy so it was a brilliant feeling.

Tony Gallimore was the first to get stuck into the champagne, because he liked a drink – in fact we were fighting to get it off him. I can just picture his big, daft face laughing. I looked at him and said, 'We're going to Wembley!' Then he turned around and said, 'I've played there before – twice!'

By this stage we had all changed our opinion about the Auto Windscreens Shield. This is exactly what the competition was for. It was for all those lads who were never going to play top flight football but here was a chance for them, playing for lower league teams, to play in a final at Wembley. And it was a dream for everyone to play at Wembley, of course it was. It was just an absolute dream.

But more importantly, what it did for Grimsby Town that season was that it gave us that momentum to do well in the league.

Suddenly, you knew as a player that if you didn't play well in the league games you would be out of the team and you wouldn't be playing at Wembley. It really concentrated our minds, I can tell you.

But it wasn't just that, the crowds came with it too and it was just like a rollercoaster, it got to the stage where we just couldn't stop winning.

Nearly all the lads in the squad in those days lived in or near Grimsby so we could sense the atmosphere and the excitement about Wembley building in the area. We had won plenty of promotions in the past but this was a different feeling. It really felt like it was a good place to be, not just in the town but in the club and among the lads. Everyone wanted to be a part of it, businesses wanted to be sponsoring games, everyone wanted to be your mate.

When you went out for a drink on a Saturday night, everyone wanted to let you in for free and people wanted to buy you a beer. It was like you had won the lottery, it was brilliant!

It was a really good time, it felt like the summer had come early because there was such a warm feeling around the place.

Once we had won the game at Turf Moor we had a couple of drinks and celebrated but then it was back to business. We had a game on the following Saturday so we said to ourselves, 'OK, let's forget about Wembley for now.' And we did. The final was another month away so we concentrated on trying to get promotion.

As we sat on the bus on the way back from that incredible night at Burnley, Wembley was very much on our minds. We were thinking to ourselves, 'We're not bothered if we win or lose! We're going to Wembley, it's going to be an unforgettable day out.'

And that's how we treated it, like a fantastic day out for us to look forward to. That was how the manager made us feel – he told us, 'Listen, whatever happens, happens. You're giving the town a great day out.' What he was telling us was, 'If you do win it, well done – but even if you don't, that's still fantastic.' Either way we couldn't lose, which made us all feel great.

Getting to Wembley was massive for a place like Grimsby, not just the club but the whole town, because they had never got there before. It was something really special for a town like that which is a bit out on a limb. People had never been to Wembley before or if they had it would have been to watch Newcastle or Manchester United or one of the other big teams – not to support their own team.

For a club of that size we had a great following away from home and this was their dream – to watch their club at Wembley.

We knew it was going to be huge. Once we won that game at Burnley, the ticket sales went through the roof. Within weeks we sold 28,000 and yet we were still asking for more. It was absolutely phenomenal.

In the final we were going to play Bournemouth and when we started to hear that they had sold 30,000 tickets as well we just got more and more excited. The size of the crowd at Wembley was going to be crazy, it had gone off the scale.

I remember talking to Tony Gallimore who had said to me that he had lost there and it was the worst thing that had ever happened to him in football. He had been to Wembley with Carlisle in the same trophy three seasons before and they had lost to Birmingham.

What made it worse was that it was a golden goal that had won it for Birmingham, the first time a Wembley final had ever been won by a golden goal. The thing was that they had only just started the idea of golden goals so when Paul Tait scored, Tony instinctively ran into his own goal, got the ball, sprinted back to the halfway line and put the ball down for the restart.

But then of course the ref said, 'What are you doing? It's a golden goal – it's all over.'

Poor old Tony. He told me not only was he disappointed that they had conceded the goal but he was so frustrated because he couldn't do anything about it. He felt like he should still have 20 minutes to play and get a goal back. After he told me that, it really made me think, 'I never want that feeling to happen to me.'

# 11

# You'll Need A Lifejacket, Son

Once we had got to the Auto Windscreens final, there seemed to be a momentum that kicked into our league performances and it got to the stage where it was almost like we couldn't lose. Even if we played badly we still won. The momentum kept us going and going and going.

Of course with a cup final there's a big sideshow away from the actual football. Before the game itself, we all needed to get suited up for example so we trooped into town to get fitted out.

That was all part of the build-up and quite exciting. However, I don't know what went wrong with my measurements but my suit was just ridiculous. I looked like a Teddy Boy. Apparently I had too long arms so they had to get a bigger jacket – but of course the jacket went down to my knees. The girl at the shop tried to take it up but she could only take it up so much because the pockets were in the way.

I remember the team photo – in fact I still look at it now and think, 'Look at the state of me! How come I'm the only one with a rubbish suit?'

We went to a place near London for three days before the final and the build-up was great, the atmosphere was really buzzing.

But when we actually trained, there was a problem. I had struggled with a hamstring injury a couple of years before and here we were, two days before the Wembley final and I felt it again on the first training session.

My first thought was, 'Oh no! I can't play.' My mind was racing as I started to think – what should I do? Should I own up and tell the manager I've done it? Then he could get someone else in to play and make sure we win the game. That would be the honest thing to do. Or am I going to be selfish and not say anything? That way I wouldn't miss out on that feeling of going out at Wembley, which was of course a boyhood dream. It was the kind of game you saw on telly.

Funnily enough I had been to Wembley as a spectator only a few weeks before to watch Middlesbrough play in the League Cup final against Chelsea – and Boro had been beaten. I was mortified. All I had wanted was for Middlesbrough to at least score a goal so we could all jump up and savour it but it never happened, they lost 2–0.

So when it was our turn to go to Wembley, what I really wanted above all else was to play and for us to score so I could see our fans go mental. When my hamstring flared up I thought it was going to take at least two weeks to get rid of it.

I mulled it over but after a while I decided I wasn't going to say anything, I was going to play. I had just bought twenty-odd tickets for my family and I wasn't going to let my family come all the way down here and not see me walk out of that bloody tunnel!

I went ahead and trained as normal but it turned out it wasn't just me with an injury niggle, Kingsley Black and Steve Livingstone were also struggling. No one knew because the three of us were all trying to keep it quiet.

We were all having our injuries iced the whole time – we were like Mr Freeze after a couple days of that sort of treatment.

In the end I had to tell the physio. I said to him we couldn't tell the manager because he would leave me out of the team but if I went to the chiropractor, he might be able to sort me out and I would be alright.

As part of our build-up, Alan Buckley told us the next day would be a bit of a fun day rather than proper training, which was good news for those of us with our secret injuries. I knew that would give me a bit of breathing space if I wasn't having to sprint anywhere that day.

After that, on the last day of training I didn't feel my hamstring and I realised I had cracked it. Fortunately my gamble had paid off and my injury didn't bother me at all during the game.

There was a party atmosphere as the game got closer and as we went down to the stadium on the bus we were all laughing and joking. It was amazing how no one seemed to be taking things all that seriously.

When we got down there, mind you, we had a bit of a shock. We got to our dressing room and my first reaction was, 'What a dive this is!' There was a sink in the corner and a little table to put your tea but that was it. Here we were at the famous Wembley at last and what a let-down it seemed to be.

We soon changed our tune though when we walked out of the dressing room, up some steps and past the toilets. That was when we saw the absolutely massive bath. Honestly, it was the size of a swimming pool and it had a giant England badge above it.

We all thought, 'Yes, that's what it's all about! I'm going in there. I'm definitely having some of that!' I asked the guy who worked in there, 'How deep does this go then, mate?'

And he just turned to me, looked me up and down and said, 'You'll be needing a lifejacket, son.'

We had all been given big blue towels with the Auto Windscreens badge on them, so my next job was to go round looking for other things to take back with me as souvenirs, 'Yes, I'm having that, and I'm having one of those.'

Alan Buckley was great at this stage. He was happy with how it was all going and he had a knack for getting all the lads relaxed. He managed us brilliantly that day because we could easily have got nervous with it being such a big day for the club.

The telly came out and there was a preview of the match with Dave Beasant on. He had played with us on loan briefly a few seasons before and there he was saying, 'All the best lads, I hope it goes really well.'

I thought it was a really nice gesture for him to go on TV and wish us good luck like that. And Alan was saying to us, 'That's who you've got backing you, lads. You need to do it today for people like that.'

By the time it got to the warm-up, the atmosphere was really building up in the stadium. It was a brilliant feeling. I had a brand new pair of boots and every time we ran across the pitch the fans gave us a massive cheer and a wave. I was enjoying it so much, I never wanted it to end. I savoured every bit of it, looking round and checking out all the sights and sounds.

When it came to the team talk, there was nothing fancy from Alan, it was the same sort of thing that he normally did. But the message he did get across was, 'No regrets. Whatever you do, don't come in thinking you froze or you panicked and wishing you could go out and do it again because you'll never get another chance again. Take your chance today. You just do your stuff and you'll win it.'

One thing we had been told beforehand was, 'Whatever you do, don't wave to your families on your way out. That's a sign of weakness. It looks like you're just there for the day out.' But, do you know what? We did it anyway – we weren't bothered!

We lined up for the national anthem and then we were all introduced to the guest of honour for the day, who was Lawrie McMenemy. Even that was a bit of a good luck omen because he was a big hero for Grimsby Town. He had only been manager there for two years in the early 1970s but he made a massive impact and won promotion. When I got introduced to him, it might as well have been the Queen as far as I was concerned.

It was such a fabulous occasion – and at that stage all I could think about was that I was going to be on telly. It was live on Sky and there was also a small matter of 62,000 there in the stadium, with fireworks going off as we walked out.

When they played the actual anthem, I could feel the hairs on the back of my neck all standing up. It was unreal. And to this day every time I hear the national anthem now for any game, I still get that feeling.

We knew Bournemouth were a good side, they were a proper footballing team like we were so we knew we were up against a side who could match us. In fact, I was expecting it to be a really entertaining game to watch.

For some reason in that final, all the action always seemed to be down one particular end – whichever team was playing with the Royal Box on their right-hand side always seemed to be on top.

In the first half we were kicking the opposite way and Bournemouth were in charge. But our fans were behind us and they were unbelievable. We didn't necessarily take as many supporters as Bournemouth but ours were louder.

When Bournemouth scored about half an hour into the first half it was one of the worst feelings I have ever known in football. There was a bit of a mix-up between Gally and our keeper which was just one of those things but when the ball ended up in the back of the net, someone might as well have taken a spear and stabbed me with it. I felt sick. I was absolutely mortified and it was made even worse by the sight of their fans going ballistic.

We got to the break and Alan was still quite calm about the situation. Bournemouth had looked dangerous and I had cleared one off the line but we had also created a few early chances, Lee Nogan had missed a couple and Kev Donovan was looking busy.

I had been getting forward a fair bit and I was still enjoying it but in the back of my mind was the nagging feeling that I just couldn't let us get beaten. The manager simply told us at half-time, 'You're better than them. You'll win – just keep going, keep going.' We went out for the second half still confident and this time we were on top.

After about 20 minutes, I remember getting the ball, doing a little one-two and cutting inside. I hit what was quite a good shot and as it flew towards the goal I really thought for a moment that it was going in until their keeper Jimmy Glass pulled off a great save and kept it out. But that was an important moment for us because it got our fans going and it lifted us.

I started to think to myself, 'Yes, I'm up for this, I'm going to have another go.' Fifteen minutes from the end, I was up in their half again and got a bit of space after another one-two and a backheel so this time I dinked a cross right to the far stick.

By this stage, Kingsley Black and Steve Livingstone had both come on as subs – they were the other two who had

The guy with the 'tache is David Hodgson, who played for Boro and was my hero as a kid. This was the first trophy I won playing for a proper side, The Priory.

My early days at Grimsby Town.

St Pius school team, 1979 – look at me leaning!

In action for Grimsby Town at Oxford in 1999. *Reproduced by kind permission of the Grimsby Telegraph*

Here I am playing at Blundell Park against Gillingham. *Reproduced by kind permission of the Grimsby Telegraph*

This is me up against Kevin Gray of Huddersfield. *Reproduced by kind permission of the Grimsby Telegraph*

My testimonial against Leeds in 1996 was to mark ten years at the club.

We all shaved our heads in 2011. *Reproduced by kind permission of the Grimsby Telegraph*

In action during the Auto Windscreens Shield final against Bournemouth at Wembley. *Reproduced by kind permission of the Grimsby Telegraph*

Celebrating our Wembley win against Bournemouth.

Harry the Haddock is in evidence as we celebrate beating Northampton in the play-off final.

Parading the trophy with me after the Wembley play-off final are Dave Smith, Peter Handyside and Lee Nogan. *Reproduced by kind permission of the Grimsby Telegraph*

Happy memories of successful seasons with Freetime Sports.

## 50
## John McDermott
**Club** Grimsby Town
**Position** Right-back
**Age** 37

Along with Oldham's David Eyres, John McDermott's performances defy the laws of human physiology. As a 37-year-old who's notched up 700 appearances in the lower leagues, he should have been bundled off to the knacker's yard a while ago; instead, he's continuing to shine for his one and only club. "There's no secret formula," he said after his second testimonial, against Hull City earlier in the season. "If you look after yourself and have the enthusiasm and desire to play, you keep on going. I've been reinvigorated since Russell Slade came to the club – even at my age!"

**David Healy**
Disgruntled Fulham fans may wonder if it's the same person, but he became the first footballer from any country to score 13 goals in a European Championship qualification campaign. And he gave £1,000 towards the erection of a George Best statue in Belfast.

**Brian Ashton**
He treats his players like adults and he's no autocrat. And, having enabled England to punch way above their weight at the rugby union World Cup, he bore some truly silly sniping by media and players with dignity.

**John McDermott**
Retired this year after spending 21 seasons as Grimsby Town's right-back. After he was substituted at Shrewsbury in the last of his 647 league appearances, play was stopped so both teams could applaud the 38-year-old off the field.

**Ivica Osim**
The Bosnian former manager of the Japan football team who had a stroke and fell into a coma. On awaking he asked: "What happened in the game?"

**Daryl Peach**
He is 35, he is from Blackpool and he collected £49,000 in Manila when he

The Wigan Wa arrested – at 5am driver James Cam

## Quotes
## the year

‘ Angelina Jolie?
on the Slimfast
Brad Pitt – well,
knock him out o
Ricky Hatton's r
on the ringside

I was honoured to be named in the Top 50 players in the Football League by *FourFourTwo* magazine in 2006.

The *Sunday Times* picked me as one of their sporting heroes of 2007.

My second testimonial against Hull was a memorable night.

Grimsby Institute team.

At the PFA with Alan Buckley and my dad.

Flanked at the PFA by Grimsby legend Dave Boylen and Fabio Capello.

My dad with a giant-sized poster of me at PFA awards ceremony.

Being interviewed by Jeff Stelling after receiving the PFA Merit Award. *Reproduced by kind permission of the PFA and the Press Association*

I'm in good company here – Ashley Young and Ryan Giggs, the other PFA winners. *Reproduced by kind permission of the PFA and the Press Association*

Coaching duties for Harrogate Town. *Reproduced by kind permission of Harrogate Town*

got away with their pre-match injuries so all three of us who might have missed out were now on the pitch together.

As my cross reached the back post, Kingsley got in a header which somehow hit the keeper and went in – we had equalised. All I remember was somehow thinking, 'I've scored!'

I knew I hadn't actually scored but as far as I was concerned I might as well have done – and it was my cross that led to the goal. I went racing off to the crowd, blowing kisses to them, I was skipping, I was going absolutely bananas!

I look back now and wonder what on earth I was doing – but that adrenalin was something I have never ever experienced except for maybe when my kids were born. Even then, this was different, I was literally shaking.

Of course, all these celebrations meant that by the time I got back to my position, I was knackered! I was sweating so much it was like I'd had a bath. Mind you, if you watch the video of the game Alan Buckley was hilarious too when we scored that goal. He got up to celebrate and was shaking his head about but he didn't really know what to do – I think more than anything it was a feeling of relief that we were still in the game.

It was all to play for now. With 90 minutes nearly up on the clock, I got the ball on the edge of their D and I dropped my shoulder on the lad who was marking me – that was a first for starters. I had never dropped my shoulder on anyone before in my life.

I remember flicking it over his foot and belting it towards the goal – and again all I could think was that it was going in. But Jimmy Glass dived and it just hit his fingertips and went out for a corner. It was only later when you watch it again on TV and see the timer in the corner of the screen that you realise just how close to the end it was. We took the corner, nothing came of it and the referee blew the final whistle.

That was a bit of a disappointment because I knew if that had gone in that would have been it – Bournemouth wouldn't have had time to go down the other end to get back into it.

Now we were into extra time – and the golden goal. Ten minutes in I got cramp to make matters worse. The golden goal rule was still quite a new thing and it made it very difficult to pace yourself in extra time because you didn't know if you were going to have to play the full half an hour or whether it was going to be all over in a minute. There was no chance of me going off though. You would have had to stretcher me off – and in any case we had used our subs because Kev Jobling had also come on.

Bournemouth had a great chance in the first period of extra time. They hit us on the break quite fast, a dangerous cross came in and I could sense little Mark Stein was right behind me. I really thought Steiny was going to head it in but I leapt up and as I jumped I just managed to nick it away from the top of his head and clear it. But when I landed – my God! My toes were like Aladdin's! They just curled up. I really couldn't believe I had such bad cramp in both calves. I didn't know how I was going to last the whole of extra time.

With only 8 minutes left, we got a corner and Kingsley whipped it in. I could see Wayne Burnett moving into a really dangerous position. I really thought he was going to score but for those few moments it was like everything was in slow motion – I just couldn't get myself to move. I felt like I was walking on the moon – meanwhile Wayne was hitting it perfectly on the side volley and, bang, it was in!

He went off like a rocket to celebrate – there was no catching him. And even then it took a few seconds to dawn on me – it was a golden goal! We had won! There was no kick off, we had actually won it!

By the time I realised it was all over, Wayne had already gone behind the goal, over the sandpit, over the barrier and he was in with the fans. By the time we got to him he was already on his way back – in fact he had almost run right past us again.

It was an amazing feeling. All the bench were on the pitch, my shirt was off, I was waving to everyone, all the flags were going. Funnily enough, by this stage, my cramp had gone – in fact I was like Carl Lewis!

I could understand why teams do concede goals straight after scoring on big occasions because the adrenalin goes right through you, your concentration levels are zero and you're knackered.

I was absolutely sapped at the end of it all but it was an immense feeling. Honestly, what better feeling was there in football? This had been a boyhood dream – and now I had done it.

To make it even better, after I had kissed everyone that I knew, an official came up to me and said, 'You are the man of the match.' To start with, I thought he was joking but he said, 'No, it's true – and there's a trophy up there for you.'

That was when I had a sudden flashback to being a teenager. 'Is it a big one?' I asked him. It was just like being a 14-year-old again! He assured me it was a big bronze thing, better than the ones we were all going to get for winning the final. Brilliant!

The guy said I was supposed to go up for the presentation second after the captain because I was the man of the match so I got in behind Paul Groves. But traditionally the keeper normally goes up second so Aidy Davison was saying, 'What are you doing? I'm second.'

I told him it was because I was getting the man of the match award but I think poor Aidy thought I was winding him up. I don't think he believed me until the official came over to tell him that I needed to go second and he had to go behind me.

For the Auto Windscreens final, all the winning team were given miniature shields but as they started handing these out, I wasn't even bothered about mine, I was more bothered about looking out for the man of the match award. Just how big was it going to be? Honestly, it was like my 14-year-old self had completely come out again.

They also ran out of the individual winners' shield trophies – we got to the last of our players and they were one short, there weren't any left. The officials said, 'Sorry, they've all gone.'

It seemed strange that they did not have enough trophies to go round – but the mystery was solved later. If you look carefully at the photos of the team celebrating on the pitch, the physio John Fraser is on it, with his son wearing a baseball cap and holding what must have been the missing trophy!

Not only that but we noticed later that the actual date of the final was wrong on the trophies. We tried to get Auto Windscreens to change it but they couldn't so we ended up taking the plates off and sending them off to have them re-done. And when the shop gave them back with the right date on they were a slightly different colour, more of a silver rather than the gold of the originals. Still, I suppose that makes them unique.

The actual trophy itself was massive when we got close enough to see it. Grovesy was really buzzing when he lifted it up and because I was second in the line, the atmosphere was still fantastic when it came to me. It was a phenomenal feeling to lift that trophy, the fans were going mental.

When I got my man of the match award my dad was nearly in tears. I was so happy for him – all my family were just behind the Royal Box, just about touching distance away, which made it really special. I had been able to see my family in the crowd as well when I was on the pitch, which was a lovely feeling.

It is crazy when you think that there were nearly 30,000 fans supporting Grimsby there that day and yet as we were dancing round the back of the goal and on to the sandy bit with the trophy in our hands, I was spotting people that I normally saw every day at home – but here we were at Wembley.

When we got back into the changing room that was when the drinking started in celebration. The poor old guy who worked in there as a steward got completely drenched – I hope they bought him a new suit afterwards because the one he had was ruined.

Alan Buckley didn't normally drink a drop but he was the first one to start knocking it back – he was going hell for leather, he was absolutely buzzing!

And then we had the famous bath. We all dived in – and I'm not kidding you, I almost did need a life jacket. For one thing I was knackered, the water was red hot and it was also about five feet deep. Add to that the champagne I had already had and suddenly I realised I couldn't get out. There I was almost fainting, thinking I was going to drown. I just didn't have the energy to get up the steps – the lads basically had to push me up them.

After we had got changed and seen our families, we were all still buzzing – and that's when we saw the real Wembley in many ways, when it was empty. Normally you don't ever see it like that.

My mate Andy Tillson, who had also played at Wembley, had told me, 'It goes too quickly. Look around and make sure you take it all in.' So I was looking around everywhere, touching every seat on our way out. I really took it all in that day.

We didn't really have much chance to have an organised party because we were still in the thick of a promotion campaign and had some important league games coming up – but as I sat back on the bus clutching my souvenir towel, I really didn't mind.

In fact, I didn't have a care in the world.

# 12

# Ali Bomaye!

After the Auto Windscreens Shield final on the Sunday, we had Carlisle away in the league on the Tuesday and we still had the job of cementing our play-off spot.

As we sat on the bus heading back home from Wembley I was sitting next to Steve Livingstone. I turned to him and said, 'Do you know what? If we had to stop today, if someone came along now and told us we had to finish playing for good – that would do me. I'd happily pack it in after what we've achieved now.'

It wasn't bad, was it? Two lads from Middlesbrough, one from Berwick Hills and one from Park End, who started off with nowt. We could certainly tell a few people who didn't think we'd make anything of ourselves that they could shove it now, couldn't we? We were like two old men there, looking back, without a care in the world.

Because of the game we had coming up on the Tuesday, there was no official party planned after winning at Wembley so when we got back to Grimsby we just got dropped off and our partners were picking us up.

But we thought we would ring up one of the pubs to see if we could sort out a little something of our own. We got in touch with the Ship Inn, in a village called Barnoldby le Beck, to see if we could have a bit of a lock-in because it was quite late by this time.

One or two of us knew the owner quite well because we'd had meals there sometimes and when we asked if we could come in and have a quick beer he was delighted to have us.

It was a lovely pub, he had a big open fire and a few of the wives and girlfriends were there so it was a perfect way to end the day. We started off just having a couple of beers but before you knew it, it was four in the morning and we were still there.

Occasionally someone would remind us that we had a game on Tuesday but by that stage our attitude was, 'We're not bothered! We'll beat them easy!'

Of course we went to Carlisle two days later and we were bloody awful. Somehow we managed to sneak a 1–0 win. That victory proved to be important because in our last two games we only drew 0–0 away at Watford and then we lost at home in the last match of the season at home to Oldham. Despite that we managed to finish third and seal our place in the play-offs.

That was when the word started going round that the team that came third never ever got promoted. And to make matters worse we were playing Fulham in the semi-finals. They were the last team we wanted at that stage because they were a good side. They had appointed Kevin Keegan as manager and had brought in some big-hitters. We would rather have played them in the final because then at least if we had lost, we would have got to Wembley again.

The first leg was away and we were going into the game not on particularly good form so when Fulham scored, it was tin hats time. We were wearing a new blue kit for the first time which was going to be our new away kit for the following season and we had felt good before the game but now we had to really dig in. Craven Cottage was quite an intimidating place to play and we never seemed to play very well there. They had players like Paul Peschisolido up front and they had a really solid back four as well so the signs at that stage weren't looking good.

But then Fulham had Paul Moody sent off and it suddenly got a little bit easier with them down to ten men. Before long Dave Smith dropped his shoulder and hit a great shot to equalise and we went into raptures. At 1–1 we all realised that we were right back in the tie and we had a great chance to go through by beating them back at our place.

That was how it finished. Keegan was fuming about the result and the sending off, which gave us a boost. What made us even more confident after that first leg was that we felt we were Keegan's bogey side when it came to playing teams he was managing. In particular, we'd had some great results against Newcastle when he was there. The year that Newcastle went up as champions to the Premier League under Keegan in 1992/93, they had had a record-breaking run of eleven consecutive league wins at the start of the season – but it was Grimsby who had beaten them to put an end to it. That was a memorable game – Jim Dobbin scored an absolute screamer late on to win it 1–0 for us in front of 30,000 Geordies at St James' Park.

In the second leg of the play-off semi-final back at Blundell Park things really went for us from quite early on. Peschisolido got himself sent off so they were down to ten men again. Then Kev Donovan scored for us again – he was a big-game player and often seemed to pop up with important goals when it mattered. At that stage we thought, 'We're going to do this!' The fans could certainly feel it.

But as the game went on, Fulham started to pile the pressure on and we were getting tired. There were a lot of last-ditch tackles going in and I cleared one off the line.

We saw out the game though and when the final whistle went that incredible wave of emotion came over us again. That Wembley buzz was back! It was only just over three weeks since we had beaten Bournemouth – and that had been Grimsby's first ever trip to Wembley in their history. Now after waiting all those years, we were going back there again already – how ridiculous was that?

We all went out that night because there was a gap before the play-off final so we could let our hair down a bit. It was mental. It was like a New Year's Eve party.

The atmosphere around Grimsby for the whole of that period was absolutely brilliant. What seemed to happen was that the Wembley buzz infected everyone in the whole town and for a couple of weeks everyone got on with each other. You didn't see any arguments or scuffles in the pubs, everyone was caught up in it all and it was like one big party.

It was unbelievable – as a player, even if I was just going to Asda I would have people coming up to me to say congratulations and have their photographs taken with me or telling me about all the members of their family that they were going to take to Wembley.

It was a phenomenal atmosphere around town but strangely enough we didn't sell as many tickets for the play-off final as we did for the Auto Windscreens Shield game. Quite why that was is hard to say. One theory was that a lot of people were saying to themselves, 'I've been once and we won. I don't want to go again and spoil the memory of the first one by seeing us get beaten this time.'

In the play-off final we were playing Northampton Town. I was actually touch and go to play at one stage. In the second leg of the semi-final against Fulham I got smashed across the head by an elbow. At first I thought I had done something to my jaw but later on it turned out it was my temple.

After that game, while we were celebrating beating them and getting back to Wembley, I didn't really think too much more about it. But three days later I noticed I was bumping into walls. I thought to myself, 'What's going on here? Am I still leathered from the party we had afterwards?'

I didn't feel well so I went to the physio and told him I was feeling dizzy. The next thing I knew I had virtually collapsed and they had me in an ambulance with an oxygen mask. I was diagnosed with delayed concussion and they said I would need ten days to recover – which put me very much in doubt for playing in the final.

I got over the worst of it fairly quickly but I was obviously desperate to play at Wembley again so every time anyone asked how I was, I said I was fine – even though I still wasn't feeling quite right.

As the game approached and we started to do interviews and so on in the build-up, you could sense that something was changing with the way Alan Buckley was treating the match. We didn't have the same party atmosphere among the players any more. This time it was serious.

We had to wear the same suits as we had worn before out of superstition. And I had to make Alan his cups of tea on the way down to Wembley as I had been doing for years. A lot of people in football are very superstitious and Alan is certainly one of them so he insisted that we stayed at the same hotel as well. It had become a tradition for me to make Alan's tea on the way to matches and once that had started there was no way he would allow it to change because it would be bad luck. Honestly, for years and years I was like a glorified tea boy for him!

The preparations for the play-off final were all the same as they had been for the Auto Windscreens Shield game against Bournemouth apart from the fact that we were much more serious in our approach and we worked more on defending set-pieces because we knew that was Northampton's strength. Aidy Davison practised a lot of corners – we knew if he came for them and collected everything in the air we would be alright.

The night before the final we were having a beautiful meal in the hotel. It was one of those posh places where the food was brought to your table under giant silver domes.

Now, Mark Lever was one the funniest lads I have ever met in football but he was also one of the smelliest. He was always trumping left, right and centre – he never made a noise, he would just gas everyone and it would linger for hours.

Unbeknown to most of us, one of the lads had nipped out to the supermarket and bought some Pedigree Chum dog food and then asked one of the chefs to secretly put it under one of the domes for Mark as a joke.

What no one was expecting was that the chef actually warmed it up first! I knew something was up because I could see Aidan Davison and Dave Smith laughing but I didn't really know what was going on.

But when the chef lifted the dome on the plate with the dog food on, the smell was absolutely evil – you could have hit your nose with a baseball bat!

It was a full plate, there must have been two tins of it, and all the jelly had melted into it. Within seconds, the revolting smell had spread right through the restaurant and the rest of the hotel – and there were some quite snooty people staying there, not just us footballers.

You should have seen Alan Buckley's face when the smell hit him – he couldn't believe what we had done!

That sort of thing went towards creating a party atmosphere and relaxing us before the final. But overall, our whole approach to this trip to Wembley was very different.

Our feeling was that we had given our fans a day out the first time round – this time it was all about us as a team. It would be great if we could win it for the fans too but this time, deep down we knew we were going to do it for ourselves.

This was more than just a cup final, this was business – it was about all the hard work we had put in all season, it was about promotion, it was about the chance to play in what was still called the First Division in those days against big, big clubs like Wolves and Sunderland.

This was our chance to get this sort of atmosphere every week, to go to these big grounds every other week. It started to sink in. We had already had a taste of victory at Wembley, we knew what it was like and we just couldn't imagine having that feeling snatched away from us.

We knew that for the play-off final, the losers didn't go up the steps to receive runners-up medals or anything like that because it wasn't like any other normal cup final. And I really wanted to go back up those steps. I really, really wanted it.

There was a major distraction for me, however. My contract was nearly up and although a new deal was in the offing, I had also been getting a bit of interest from other clubs.

I got a call at the hotel from my agent Mel Stein telling me not to sign a new deal with Grimsby yet because Ipswich were interested in signing me. Ipswich were in the division above us at the time, the one Grimsby were hoping to get promoted to, and they were always the sort of club who were looking to push on even higher. I liked the way they played their football too – they had some good players under George Burley.

It was the kind of phone call that was very flattering to receive but to be honest it wasn't exactly great timing just before such an important game at Wembley. I sat there in my hotel room thinking this play-off final could be my last ever game for Grimsby. I tried to put it out of my head and focus on the football.

When the day of the game arrived and we went out onto the pitch before kick-off to sample the atmosphere, things did seem different to the Bournemouth game in the Auto Windscreens Shield final just three weeks earlier. Behind the goal there were more gaps among our following because we didn't have as many fans as we had before.

We still took something like 18,000 but Northampton brought an amazing number of supporters with them so the crowd overall was the same sort of size as it had been before – well over 60,000 altogether. That is a lot of people when you're used to playing in front of tiny crowds at places like Southend and Brentford. The atmosphere for the second Wembley game was just as good and even though our fans were outnumbered, they seemed louder than Northampton's and that just helped us feel even more confident.

My concussion started to kick in again a little bit as I watched the youngsters playing a warm-up game on the Wembley pitch before our match. But luckily enough it wore off again and I was fine by the time we kicked off.

The manager was confident that we were by far the better footballing side and if we played our football we would win. We had been to Wembley before and won so there was no reason not to go and do it again.

Buckley's team talk was totally different to how it had been three weeks earlier. He wouldn't let us relax and have a joke – he drilled it into us that this time it was business.

As we were waiting to go out onto the pitch Northampton came out into the tunnel to join us and although they were mostly big lads we were pretty sure we had them sussed. They were a bit of a long ball team although they were very good at it. They had some good players but they had a very direct style of play, with John Gayle up front. One of their most dangerous players was Chris Freestone who was light and quick – we were warned about him. Even though we knew we were more of a footballing team, Northampton were efficient at what they did. We were confident in our own ability as a footballing side but we knew it was going to be a tough game.

As the two teams were standing there waiting to go out onto the pitch, something strange happened that somehow gave us an extra lift just before kick-off. It was Kevin Jobling who started it. He was a good player, he could play anywhere, but he was also the club clown in a lot of ways. From out of the blue, he started singing this Muhammad Ali song, 'Ali bomaye! Ali bomaye!' It was what the local fans chanted at his famous fight against George Foreman in Zaire in 1974, the so-called 'Rumble in the Jungle'.

Kev was chanting, 'Ali bomaye! Ali bomaye!' and the next minute Livvo started doing it as well. Big Aidan Davison, our goalkeeper, was next to join in, waving his hands and jumping up and down. Before long the whole line of us were bouncing up and down with it too and the noise of it was going right down the tunnel.

Bear in mind, there's not much room in that tunnel and the opposition are right on your shoulder.

Alan Buckley turned round and said, 'What the bloody hell's going on here?' But we didn't need to explain ourselves because as we glanced over and looked at the Northampton players, we knew they were beaten before we'd even gone out on to the pitch. The Northampton lads looked at us as if to say, 'We're playing lunatics here.'

That Ali chant had got a few of our lads laughing and taken the pre-match tension of the moment away for us – but we had also psyched out the opposition. When you heard even our winger Kingsley Black chanting it, that just gave you a special feeling. He was like a saint who went round with a halo on his head – yet even he was joining in.

And deep down, I think the Northampton players knew they didn't have the same togetherness that we did. Looking back, those players were a great set of lads – there wasn't one of them that you wouldn't happily enjoy going out for a pint with. There really wasn't a single bad lad among them.

We looked across to the opposition and thought to ourselves it was just a matter of how many we were going to score. It felt like there was no chance of us losing – that's what that Ali chant had done for our confidence.

The manager reminded me as we were going out, 'You're playing against a lad called Carl Heggs. He's their ball player so if you keep him quiet, we'll win.' I knew Heggs was a good player – tricky, tall, and quick so suddenly I felt a little bit of extra pressure on my shoulders.

But right from the first minute we didn't seem fazed by anything. We defended a few corners but we never seemed in any danger. If you look back now at the video of the game, you can clearly see the contrast between the two teams. We did what we did best, they did what they did – and we were superior.

During the game, I managed to blank out all thoughts of the interest from Ipswich and I felt I nailed Heggs during the game. As a result he didn't really do much at all over the 90 minutes. I didn't have a particularly great game going forward because I felt my job was to look after him so I stuck to that task.

When you look over the two Wembley games, I actually played better in the second game, I thought, even though it was in the first one that I was the man of the match.

Our all-important goal came midway through the first half from Kev Donovan once more. He was normally a right-winger but on this occasion he floated in off the left and rounded the keeper. As he was shaping to put it into the net, it was like time had stood still again – you just wanted him to smash it!

When it went in, it was a great feeling again but this time it was different – it wasn't euphoria, it was more like relief that we were winning against a team we felt we should be beating.

Once we had gone 1–0 in front we felt it was all over even though there was still more than an hour left. We weren't playing particularly well but we just didn't think there was any way Northampton would score against us except maybe from a set piece.

At half-time, the manager maybe sensed that because he was desperate not to allow us to relax. He knew how close we were to winning it. His team talk was uplifting – he had an aura about him at times like that which meant no one wanted to make a mistake. You didn't want to get the Buckley stare so you did your job right.

When we got a penalty in the second half we really thought that would be game over but Kev Donovan missed his chance to make it 2–0 and of course we were then a bit worried that Northampton would get a psychological lift from that let-off.

But it never came. Paul Groves smashed one against the crossbar and it felt like we were pretty much outplaying them even though we were only 1–0 up.

The minutes ticked by with only that slender one-goal advantage and when the final whistle went, it was a really mixed emotion for me. That was the moment when it hit me that it could be all over for me at Grimsby. The party atmosphere at Wembley was sensational again but as I was waving to the fans I was also thinking this was me maybe waving goodbye to them. And yet no one really knew about it apart from me and my agent.

In some ways it would have been a great way to finish my career at the club like that, on a massive high – they do say it's best to go out at the top. But at the same time it did take a bit of the shine off it for me, if I'm being honest.

After we went up for the presentation and got all our medals, we were going round the pitch celebrating with our fans and all of a sudden I saw six of my mates right at the front.

I happened to have the trophy in my hands at the time, so for some reason I just passed it over to them. I don't know what I was thinking – I then quickly realised, 'Hang on, they could run off with it!'

Fortunately I managed to get it back safely but that's the kind of daft thing you do in the euphoria of the moment. It would have been just my luck if it had disappeared and ended up at a car boot sale.

It was when we started to have the official photos taken and they were playing 'We Are the Champions' that I began to relax and enjoy things a bit more.

The party after that game was quite something. Alan Buckley doesn't normally have more than half a pint but for once he was really going for it. His head was buried inside the trophy necking champagne. After a while, his wife had to intervene, 'Alan, I think you've had enough!' As you can imagine, he took a bit of banter from the lads, 'Taxi for Buckley!'

As he stumbled off, we suddenly realised we had missed a trick because he was in such a state we could have really got our own back on him for all the stick he used to give us – especially about the clothes we wore, which he used to hate.

The lads did like to wind up Alan a little bit most days but deep down we all really admired him and would have run through a brick wall for him.

As well as Alan, the lads were over the moon for Bill Carr who was the chairman of Grimsby Town at the time. We would have played for him alone. Bill was a top, top man and he really looked after us that year. He invited all the lads round to his house for parties after games and even though he was quite a wealthy guy he treated the players as if we were his best mates. In fact, the whole board were fantastic at that period and that feeling of togetherness went right through the club.

Looking back, if we had been given the choice of which of those two Wembley games we would have most wanted to win, obviously it would have been the second one because that got us promotion which was so important. But we were greedy. We wanted to win them both and we knew we were capable of doing that.

The Mariners have been back to Wembley since and also to the Millennium Stadium but none of those games was anything like as memorable. They lost all three, the first at Cardiff in the League Two play-off final, the second at Wembley in the final of the Johnstone's Paint Trophy (the latest name for the Auto Windscreens competition) and then most recently they were beaten on penalties by Wrexham in the FA Trophy Final. That spring of 1998 was a golden era for the club, the kind which only comes round once in a lifetime.

As things turned out, I didn't get the move to Ipswich after all. They rang me a few times after the play-off final and said they had decided to try to sign a player who was coming down from the Premier League instead of me – but if they couldn't agree a deal for him then they would still take me.

Funnily enough, it was my old team-mate Gary Croft who they signed instead. I had played with him at Grimsby before he moved on to Blackburn and did quite well there.

I also had Bradford City interested in me as well – Paul Jewell was very keen on signing me. But I was told that the dressing room atmosphere wasn't too good at that time. One or two people rang me to say the team spirit wasn't great.

Alan Buckley sat me down and said, 'Look, give me a year in this division and then you go if you still want to. But give me a year to prove that we want to go places.' He was very good at trying to sweet-talk players and I was happy, I got a good deal out of it – but he had to be because Jewell was very persistent. He was begging me to go there and offering me a four-year deal. I was being offered something that was worth about £80,000 or £90,000 more to me but I didn't take it.

Out of all the chances I had to move in my career, that's the one where I'm closest to regretting not taking it – we did OK at Grimsby that season, finishing mid-table, but Bradford were runners-up and went up into the Premier League.

It wasn't a lack of ambition on my part because I honestly thought we were going to finish above them anyway. I felt we had a much better team spirit at Grimsby and that Bradford were more a collection of good individual players. So if I had decided to move, I would have been mainly motivated by getting more money. I was comfortable where I was at Grimsby, I was in the team and enjoying my football – and that seemed more important.

Another factor in my decision to stay at Blundell Park was that Bradford had some quite big names, people like Peter Beagrie, who was very influential in the dressing room.

I will be honest and admit that in a way I was in awe of people like that and I didn't want to be intimidated by that kind of atmosphere, which is what had happened earlier in my career.

Of course, Peter later came to play at Grimsby briefly right at the end of his career and it turns out he is one of the nicest lads I have ever met in football. He is a top man, a really funny guy and it made me think, 'What the hell were you doing being in awe of someone like him? Maybe I messed up there making that decision not to go to Bradford.' And he's a Middlesbrough lad as well, of course!

But you can't really regret anything in football – I went on to win other things with Grimsby which I wouldn't have done if I had moved on.

For a time Watford were also sniffing around after me so it was a bit galling to see them get promoted to the Premier League the same season as Bradford. And then Ipswich went up the following year.

That meant there were three teams who had all gone up into the Premier League, all of which I could possibly have been part of – and here I was still at Grimsby.

But you know what? I was happy to be there – we were in the First Division and we all really enjoyed the ride while it lasted. We had a run of five seasons where we punched well above our weight and played some really good football, just as we had done in Alan Buckley's first spell.

# 13

# Bombing On

It was a very sad day for me personally when Bill Carr stepped down as chairman in 1999 – in my eyes he was Mr Grimsby Town. If we hadn't had a manager, the players would all have played for him. If he ever popped his head round the corner before a match and said, 'Will you win for me today, lads?' it drove us on because even though we wanted to win anyway, we would really try even harder to do it for him.

From the day that he left, the club started to crumble slightly for me. Bill stayed around as a presence at the club for quite a few years but it wasn't the same. There was standing room only at his funeral in 2004, that's a measure of how popular he was.

Despite the memorable double Wembley success that Alan Buckley had brought only two years earlier, the new board wanted even more. In August 2000, Buckley left the club for a second time – this time he was sacked, only two games into the new season. Even those who had wanted a change of manager were bemused by the timing of it. No one could understand why Alan was sacked after two games of a new season – if he was going to be sacked, it would have made more sense to have done it at the end of the previous season so the new man would have had the whole of the summer to shape his squad.

We had John Cockerill as caretaker manager for a brief spell. Cockers was given the caretaker job a couple of times but he never got the role permanently. We will never know how he might have done – in many ways he was perfectly suited to the job because he was very popular with the fans and he had done a fantastic job with the youth team.

I have never really spoken to him about why he maybe didn't fancy it – perhaps he didn't think he had enough contacts in the game because he had been in the RAF and played for quite a part of his career with non-league teams like Stafford Rangers and Boston FC. It was a shame because he was from a really strong footballing family – his brother Glenn went on to have a very successful career at Southampton and their dad Ron played nearly 300 times for Grimsby in the 1950s and 1960s.

Ron was a great man who is sadly no longer with us. I had the privilege of meeting him quite a few times and he was just a lovely person. You could tell when he came in the dressing room that he was old school but he was also a legend with the fans.

Continuity used to be the norm at most clubs including Grimsby but football in general changes and not many clubs now seem to maintain that policy of bringing through ex-players who are schooled in how they want the club to be managed and how they want the team to play. Liverpool were famous for the way their boot room used to produce a succession of new managers from Bob Paisley to Joe Fagan to Ronnie Moran but even they have changed these days.

The board probably felt that Alan had taken them as far as he could whereas the new manager they brought in – Lennie Lawrence – was someone with better contacts in the game and more potential to make the most of the new TV money that was coming into football.

The fans were spoilt in some ways by the football we played under Alan. I don't think that style of football will ever be repeated at that club. Talk about Arsenal playing one-touch football, give-and-go passing around the box, that's exactly what we were doing week in and week out. You only have to look back at videos of that era – and there are plenty of clips on YouTube these days. We sometimes got the same sort of criticisms that Arsenal have had over recent years, that we were passing the ball too much and trying to walk the ball into the back of the net. Some fans said we weren't getting round behind teams and putting in crosses from the byline – but we didn't need to do that because of the way we played. And this wasn't Arsenal, this was Grimsby – we were really punching above our weight.

Alan was like a father figure to us all so it's great for me to still keep in touch with him. I often see him at events where he's a guest speaker. They are great nights and he sometimes tells stories about things that went on behind-the-scenes that you didn't hear about at the time as a player.

He wasn't a great one for doing his homework on the opposition though. Alan would get the dossier on the opposing team, toss it on the table and say to the players, 'Right, read it if you want but I'm not bothered if you don't. We're not playing Real Madrid – it's all about us, how we play and how well we pass the ball.'

Lennie Lawrence was the complete opposite. He would go through all the other team's weaknesses and work on those with all of his players. He realised that football was changing and the advent of technology meant you could really analyse the game and make a difference by being as thoroughly prepared as possible.

Lennie looked at Grimsby as a club and came to the conclusion that one of the few areas where we couldn't compete with other bigger teams was our fan base because we were playing sides like Nottingham Forest, Wolves and Sheffield Wednesday who could attract crowds of 20,000 – we never had that at Blundell Park, we might get 4,000 or 5,000. We had great fans but in smaller numbers and that was one of the only things that we had no control over. But in every other area he left nothing to chance.

When Lennie first came to the club, he gathered all the players together on the pitch and introduced himself to us in what sounded like a broad Cockney accent. The first thing he said to us was, 'Alright, lads. Now, the first thing I want you all to know is that me and Dario Gradi are the two managers who've sold on the most players in our time.' My initial reaction was one of disbelief. I just thought he was going to get rid of the whole lot of us. Then Lennie said, 'And by the way, I can't stand spivs.'

We were amazed – we thought he was the one who was the biggest spiv of the lot. He came across like a typical Cockney wide boy. We also thought he was a dead ringer for Mr Burns from *The Simpsons* so that became one of his nicknames. He looked like him and walked like him too.

The last thing he said to us when he first met us was, 'If you do all right by me, I'll do all right by you. But, I warn you, you've got to be able to run.'

For his first game in charge, Lennie decided to play three at the back, with me and Dave Smith as wing-backs. He said to me before the game, 'I know Dave but I don't really know much about you. You're more defensive than Dave whereas he's more like a winger being moved back to wing-back. So I want him bombing on more than you, you can just sit deeper.'

I just looked at him and thought, 'You haven't seen us play a single game, have you? I'm the "bomber on" and Dave ain't!'

When it came to the game, my instinct was, 'Bollocks to Lennie. I can't just sit at the back the whole game bored out of my skull. I'll just play my natural game.' So I bombed on and helped set up a goal and Lennie was honest enough to say to me afterwards, 'I think I got that wrong, Macca, don't you? From now on, you can bomb on and Smudger can stay back.'

From then on I got on with Lennie extremely well. It takes a special kind of person to own up to their mistakes – that's the way you learn. Plenty of managers in that situation would never have admitted they were wrong.

I have got so much respect for Lennie because what he did was to bring something into the club which we had never had before. He was as old school as they come in some ways but he dragged that club into the new age of football, a new approach to training, diet and everything else. He knew that football had moved on and other clubs had already moved on with it but Grimsby were still in the old school bracket until he came.

One of the things he introduced in training was quick feet. When he first mentioned that, some of us were bemused. 'Quick feet? What's that, learning dance steps? What's all this about?' We really didn't understand what he was on about to begin with. As well as putting cones out, he would bring ladders to training and put those out on the training ground.

'Right, lads, today we're going to do some ladder work,' he would say. The first time he did it, we looked at each other in confusion because we really thought he meant step ladders to begin with and couldn't work out how that would help our football.

Nowadays they're a standard part of training, with ladders laid out on the ground for players to do drills to improve their footwork, jumping in and out of the rungs. But at the time it was all new to us – and at first, it was a disaster for me personally. I just could not do them at all – even though I was just about the fastest player at the club.

I had the quickest feet of anyone when it came to running in a straight line but as soon as those ladders came out it was like I had diving boots on. Whenever I tried it, I knocked everything flying. Lennie would wipe the tears of laughter from his eyes and say, 'What are you doing, Macca? You're ruining my session.'

To be honest, after a while it started to get to me a bit. I began to feel a bit embarrassed about not being able to do it so every time Lennie said, 'OK, lads, it's quick feet time', I would groan and think, 'Oh no, here we go again. What are we doing this for? You don't do this in a game of football.'

I even started to try to come up with excuses as to why I couldn't do it. But by the end of the season by sheer perseverance I was really rapid at ladder work – I could go in and out of them as fast as anyone. Lennie said to me, 'If you could have seen yourself doing these three months ago, you'd have laughed your head off.'

The ladder work was only one aspect of the training drills he introduced before he even brought the ball into it – and once I had got used to them, I loved them.

We were in a bit of a relegation battle in our first season under Lennie. One of the hardest games I ever remember playing in my whole career was QPR away in March 2001 – they were scrapping for their lives too and ended up going down whereas we finished four points clear in eighteenth. But that afternoon at Loftus Road I barely got out of our eighteen-yard box in the entire 90 minutes.

They weren't a bad side despite their league position because they had players like Gavin Peacock, Leon Knight and Chris Kiwomya and it was pretty much tin hats time for us for the whole game. We had Danny Coyne in goal and I'm not kidding you, he was like a cat that day. If he hadn't pulled off about twenty great saves, we would have been dead and buried long before the end. But it was one of those games where we got a free kick late on, pumped it into the box and Paul Groves headed it in for the winner.

The summer of 2001 was Lennie's first pre-season with us at Grimsby and it turned out to be his last one as well. He took us to Malmo on a pre-season tour, which was quite an experience, one the players enjoyed so much that we went back again the following year when Paul Groves had taken over as manager. We had various new faces who came with us to Sweden, people like Phil Jevons, Kevin Ellison and Danny Coyne, and the trip to Malmo worked really well for team bonding.

Before the Malmo trip we went to the Lilleshall National Sports Centre in Shropshire for two days for some intensive training sessions and some fitness tests and Lennie told us anyone who failed their test wouldn't be going to Sweden.

Drinking was strictly banned for the two days we were there but we weren't having that – even though Lilleshall is pretty much in the middle of nowhere. Tony Gallimore, Wayne Burnett, Steve Livingstone and myself sneaked out of the hotel and got a taxi into town.

We got ourselves into a local pub and ended up absolutely steaming by the end of the night – we were really mixing our drinks that night too for some reason – Guinness, red wine, the lot, you name it. We crept back in about six in the morning, had hardly any sleep and when we got up again my head was really thumping – the last thing I needed was more of these fitness tests but that's exactly what was lined up for us first thing in the morning.

And worse than that, it was blood tests first. Our faces dropped when we heard this – all we could think was, 'Oh no, we're gonna get rumbled now for sure!' I sidled up to the guy doing the testing and asked innocently, 'Er, you're not doing blood tests for alcohol, are you?' He replied, 'Oh no, we're just checking your iron.' So I couldn't help bursting out, 'Well, ours should be sky high, we've just had about fifteen pints of Guinness each!'

We got away with that one but Livvo had something else on his mind as well. He knew he had a dodgy calf but had kept quiet about it because he was desperate to come with us on the Sweden trip, regardless of whether he would be fit enough to play or not. Sure enough, just as we were coming down the steps from the plane at Malmo Airport, he was clutching his calf. We had barely even been landed a couple of minutes and he was injured already. Lennie was livid.

'I don't believe it. It'll be just like being on holiday for you now. We can't take you back. That's just typical,' he said. Meanwhile, Livvo was beaming all over his face. He turned to me and gave me a big thumbs-up, 'Brilliant!'

Immediately Livvo was pestering Tony Gallimore to go out on the first night we were there. Gally was a bit dubious, 'We're not allowed out, there's a game tomorrow.' But Livvo was adamant, 'No, no, the boss won't mind, we won't be drinking, we'll just be having a look around the place.'

Gally didn't take much persuading because the next thing I knew he had all his going-out gear on – mind you, it was a brown Boss jumper that looked more like a potato sack than anything I would be seen dead in. I was sharing with Gally of course but he promised me he was only going out for an hour and would stick to drinking water. It was nearly breakfast time by the time that he finally crashed back into our room – so much for not waking me up. Gally looked completely leathered as he said to me, 'I tell you what, Macca, that water's strong!'

We had training first thing as well as a game later on so I was really worried about how Gally was going to get through it. Yet somehow he was right at the front of the pack when it came to running and you could tell Lennie was impressed with his sharpness. I knew he was still steaming though and I was amazed the manager couldn't smell the booze on his breath. We played the first match of our tour and we were rubbish – in fact, Gally was about the only one of us who looked decent.

Before our next game, Lennie gave us a bit of time off. There was a big square in the centre of Malmo which was where all the bars were and where all the serious drinking went on. Lennie said to us, 'Right, you've got training in the morning but the rest of the day is yours. However, I'm going to the square and I do not want to see any of you in the square, understood?'

We had been warned. But Gally's reasoning was simple, 'He said he didn't want to see us in the square, didn't he? But he didn't say anything about the bars outside the square, did he?'

Come on, then! It was party time, I tell you – we spent nearly the whole of the rest of our time there drinking in the bars that were in all the streets around the outside of the main square.

Just about the only time we weren't there was when someone piped up that there was a nudist beach in Malmo and we should go and take a look. Several of us took a walk down there – plenty of people went down there with all their gear on, that was no problem, but Wayne Burnett decided to take his camera with him and was snapping loads of pictures. Not surprisingly, people were furious. But the biggest shock of all came when we came over one particular sand dune – and there was Tony Gallimore, stark bollock naked, cigarette in one hand, bottle of beer in the other.

He greeted us with, 'Alright, lads! How're you doing?' We asked him what the hell he was playing at but he seemed perplexed and said he had heard some of the lads talking about coming down to the nudist beach so here he was.

'We were only coming down here to have a look – not be part of it!' I told him. 'Lennie's only about 200 yards behind us – if he sees you like this, he'll kill you!'

That finally stirred him into action and the last we saw of Gally was him sprinting away to safety with his clothes tucked under his arm, still with his fag and beer in his hand and his bollocks swinging from side to side.

It wasn't just the nudist beach that confirmed what we had all been told about the Swedes. While we were in Malmo, there was a couple in one of the hotel rooms opposite us but about four floors down who were always getting it on in full view of everyone. The lads often watched them at it. I am sure they knew people could see them and were playing on it a bit because every morning we used to get a performance.

One morning some of the lads were watching them from our window where you got a full-on view and Gally was shouting a bit of vocal encouragement, 'Go on, my son!'

But when the bloke suddenly looked up, it must have startled Gally and his fags started to slip out of his pocket towards the open window. Gally reached forward to grab them and in a split second he had disappeared out of the window – four floors up. Fortunately, they had windows in the hotel which opened inwards with a vertical bar in the middle and somehow Gally had grabbed the bar and swung right round and back into the room the other side.

I was in a daze – I could barely believe what I had just seen! He could so easily have fallen out of that window, plunged fifty feet and he would have been killed. But Gally was oblivious to what might have happened – in fact, he was full of himself, 'Did you see that?! I even caught my fags!'

It was preying on my mind all day and later on I started trying to get across to him just how serious it could have been. I said, 'I can't believe what happened there, you could be dead, you know?' But when I turned round he was fast asleep – typical Gally. He didn't worry, he just got on with things.

I really enjoyed our trips to Malmo more than any others; they were great for team bonding. And yet Lennie had absolutely slaughtered us for our performances when he took us there.

He said: 'You lot have come over here, you've got pissed the whole time and you wouldn't beat a Ryman League team the way you've played. You can't pass the ball, you can't defend – you'll all be sold, I'm telling you, so I can get some better players in.'

Lennie was spot on really but he maybe didn't realise just how much we were all drinking while we were there – no wonder we didn't play very well. To be honest, it felt like an end-of-season piss-up to Magaluf rather than a pre-season tour that was supposed to be getting us in shape.

However badly we had played in Sweden though, there seemed to be a beneficial effect thanks to the team bonding because we went on a great run at the start of the league season and before you knew it, we were top of the table.

# 14

# Crazy Creatine Gang

Despite everything that went on in Malmo, Lennie did get us really fit for the league season. He brought in a fitness guy from the Lilleshall National Sports Centre who started us on creatine supplements. I enjoyed that year with Lennie, I really did, he really looked after us. We took this creatine in liquid form and I felt great on it, although it didn't necessarily suit everyone – you had to take lots of fluid with it so it did seem to lead to some problems with water retention. Every now and then you might get a calf strain too but it suited me.

At the start of 2001/02 our philosophy was to really have a go at the opposition and if we got beaten, well at least we knew we had given it a go. And what happened was that we found ourselves mugging teams – we would go into the lead, sometimes spend a lot of the game under the cosh but end up winning 1–0. And in the last 15 minutes it would be the other team who were flagging whereas we would be getting our second wind.

We did have some young players coming in like Jonny Rowan and Danny Butterfield – whether it was their influence or the creatine having an effect, I don't know, but it certainly felt good to be riding high at the top of the First Division.

We also shaved our heads that season so we looked mental, like the Crazy Gang. We were really ruffling a few feathers and Lennie said to us, 'There's always one team that nobody fancies who gets into the play-offs and gets promoted – why can't it be us?'

We were all convinced it could be us too – we had real belief because we had superior fitness, we knew what we were doing and we looked the part. We weren't just fit, we actually looked fit. All our lads seemed to look wiry yet powerful.

Lennie instilled a sense of belief in us so that we really started to think that what he said was going to happen would actually happen. We were a team of battlers that season and we got a lot of our points by hanging in there in some games and believing in ourselves. We ran other teams into the ground.

There was a game at home to Barnsley at the start of September when we beat them 1–0, yet it could have been 30–0 to Barnsley, they had so many chances. And that win put us top of the league – we were in dreamland.

A week later we went to Coventry City, beat them at their ground and their manager Gordon Strachan was sacked a couple of days later. They say that more managers have been sacked after losing to Grimsby than any other team. As we were warming up at Highfield Road before the match, doing our quick feet drills, I looked across and I could see the Coventry players and their fans were watching us. It never happened to me again in my career but at that point, I could tell that other teams and other fans were looking at us and thinking, 'This is the team to beat. They're top of the league and they're going up.' It was as if we had an aura about us, being top of the league, and teams like Coventry saw us – little old Grimsby! – as a club to look up to.

Lennie introduced us to a proper approach to sport science for the first time, it was a whole new world for most of us who had been at Grimsby for a while.

As I have said, Lennie was an old school manager in lots of ways but he was also quite modern as well because he brought in quite a lot of the new scientific approach to football that was beginning to take off then. He wasn't massive on tactics, in fact sometimes his team talks were very simplistic, 'Let's go for it, get an early goal and then keep the opposition quiet for the rest of the game.'

Lennie's new approach included all kinds of other evaluations including blood tests like the ones we had at Lilleshall before the Malmo trip as well as the fitness testing that you would expect as standard these days. He and his team started to analyse exactly what we ate and drank too. For a long time, as a footballer you might have had a cup of tea and bag of crisps as part of your pack-up for an away match but suddenly everything was transformed and we were given water and isotonic drinks. What we ate and when we ate all came under scrutiny and we had to start to take notice of the different food groups we were eating, carbohydrates and so on.

It was nothing drastic really but it seemed like rocket science to us at the time. And the great thing was that all the lads bought into it – if only three of four players had done, it just wouldn't have worked in the same way. But Lennie convinced even someone like me who was already 30 by the time he started. My attitude could easily have been, 'I'm doing OK as it is. What do I need these new-fangled ideas for?'

I did buy into it like everyone else and I'm convinced that Lennie's methods put three or four years on to my career, which I'll always be grateful to him for. Pretty soon, every club in football had adopted this more scientific approach.

You can't knock Alan Buckley for his achievements at Grimsby Town but looking back, you would have to say the club was a bit behind the times under him. He really was old school, much more so than Lennie. Alan once told me that when he first started as Lincoln City's manager he met their fitness coach on the training ground and asked him what he was doing. The coach told him he was just about to start doing quick feet work and Alan's response was, 'Quick's the right word – you've got 5 minutes.' Alan wanted to be in charge of everything that went on in training, not hand some of it over to a fitness coach.

When Lennie came to Grimsby, he had made quite a reputation for himself at various clubs like Charlton, Middlesbrough, Bradford and Luton but he was mainly known as a survivor so we thought he was going to drag us down. How wrong we were because he transformed Grimsby Town beyond recognition in the relatively short time he was there.

I liked Lennie a lot but you had to be fit – he didn't like injured players. If you came out of the dressing room and turned right to go training, he was happy. But if you turned left to go to the physio's room to get some treatment, he wouldn't speak to you. He once said to me, 'You're alright by me, Macca, you always seem to turn right.'

Lennie wasn't interested in you if you were getting treatment, he only wanted people who could do the business for him on the pitch. I still speak to Lennie today and have used him as a reference when I have applied for jobs in football. He is not everyone's cup of tea but I rate him as a top man.

One thing about him was that he looked after his players, which not all managers do – some of them are more keen on looking out for their own interests. Lennie spent quite a lot of money but he made sure plenty of it went to the players because he believed in us and felt we deserved to be rewarded for our efforts. He was just about the only manager I worked under who gave me a proper pay rise.

When Lennie arrived there was a bonus system in place at Grimsby that hadn't changed for about twenty years. He immediately ripped it up and said, 'No, we're not having that.' He came up with a system where you got proper incentives for the team doing well. He had a new clause inserted into our contracts that meant if we stayed up, each player got a certain amount per point as a bonus, depending on how many games they had played. I was a regular that season so it worked out that at the end of the year I got a bonus of £16,500 on top of my regular salary for finishing only a few places above the bottom of the league. That was more than I would have got as a bonus if we had won the league under the previous system.

There were other seasons earlier in my career when we won promotion and I only got a paltry amount like £250. When details of this went in the newspapers, they nicknamed it our 'bonus ball', which, not surprisingly, didn't go down too well with the fans, however.

There was a little bit of bad feeling when it leaked out exactly how much certain players were getting as a bonus for avoiding relegation. We felt it was wrong for individual players to be named like that – it upset some of the fans because they felt we were already being paid handsomely enough as it was. That was true, I was better paid under Lennie than at any other time in my career. But the club were getting money at this stage from ITV Digital's deal to show Football League games so why shouldn't the players get a share of it?

Lennie looked after his players when it came to contracts as well. When I was due a new deal he told me to go home and think of a number, then come back and see him – but he would tell me what I was getting. I went home and tried to think of an amount that I thought was really high because I thought I might as well make the most of the TV money that was coming in. When I went in to see Lennie I had a figure in my head – but before I had a chance to say anything, he stopped me and said, 'Don't say anything. I'm going to tell you what you're getting anyway.'

He slipped me a piece of paper and the amount written on it was even higher than I was going to ask for – £500 a week more! I almost fell off my chair in amazement but somehow I kept my composure and said, 'Can I have until tomorrow to think about it?' It was all I could do to stop myself punching the air as I walked out of his office.

In the corridor was one of the other lads who was waiting to go in and see him and I said, 'Quick, get in there! Lennie's lost the plot; he's splashing the cash all over the place! I think I might go in tomorrow and tell him I'll need another £200 on top of that.'

When I did go back in to see Lennie the next day, the first thing he said was, 'I hope you've not come back here to ask for more because I can tell you right now, you're not getting it.' I bottled it and said, 'No, no, boss, of course not, I'm happy with that. I love this club.'

I could have added that I loved him even more for giving me such a good deal – I almost grabbed the contract from him in my eagerness to sign it in case he took it away from me again. I probably earned as much in that two-year deal as I did in the rest of my career put together. The tax man must have loved me for those two years.

We did have some great results under Lennie for a while and not just in the league – we also had a memorable game at Anfield when we knocked Liverpool out of the League Cup with Phil Jevons getting the winner in extra time. They had a strong side out as well, with players like Jamie Carragher, Gary McAllister, Danny Murphy, Emile Heskey and Jamie Redknapp all in their team.

When we were flying in the league under Lennie, we had a very consistent starting line-up because we didn't seem to have many injuries – maybe that was down to the fitness regime or even the fact that Lennie hated players to be injured.

It didn't last though and when our form tailed off, we began to slide down the league table. Lennie got sacked halfway through what was his second season and Paul Groves took over as manager just after Christmas 2001.

Lennie had spent a fair bit of money on bringing in players including quite a few foreign imports – there was a Chinese lad called Zhang Enhua, a Dutch midfielder called Menno Willems and a couple of Scandinavians.

We had a Danish centre-forward called David Nielsen who was a cracking player and very strong in home games, although he tended to be something of a passenger in away matches.

Zhang was a lovely fella, one of the most generous guys I have come across in my career, but he didn't speak a word of English and it was hard communicating with him. You forget that on the pitch players do need to make themselves understood to each other regardless of what nationalities are out there on the same team. As a full-back I would be saying things to him like 'push up' and he would do the opposite and drop back. Then he would inadvertently play opposition strikers onside and it would cost us goals.

He really took to the place and the fans loved him. He quickly became a bit of a cult figure just because it seemed so exotic having a Chinese international playing for Grimsby, I suppose. Don't get me wrong, he was a terrific player as well, mind you.

He was a great lad and very down to earth even though there would often be film crews following him around doing reports for Chinese TV. Zhang was a regular for the Chinese national side, went to the 2002 World Cup after he left Grimsby and scored some important goals for us.

It was rumoured he was on very big wages which didn't bother me personally at all but people did feel a bit uneasy about the entourage he brought with him. He had an interpreter with him and his own cook and people did wonder how much all that might be costing. The word around the dressing room was that Zhang got himself into trouble at the rented house where he was living for smoking fish in his garage and stinking the whole house out.

It was a shame to see Lennie go – but worse was to follow. The club suffered financially after he left mainly because ITV Digital collapsed in 2002, leaving lots of Football League clubs in debt. Clubs like Grimsby had budgeted for getting their fair share of the millions of pounds that they were supposed to be receiving from ITV Digital. A lot of the cash just didn't materialise in the end.

I was a bit down when I heard the news that Lennie was going – but when he came to see all the players to say goodbye, he was as bubbly as ever. He came in and said, 'Lads, I've been given the sack, but that's football. It's been a pleasure, see you all later.' And off he went with his Mr Burns walk.

After Paul Groves took over as manager we at least managed to steady the ship enough to avoid relegation. He brought in a couple of really good players on loan from Charlton – Andy Todd, who was the son of Colin Todd and had also played for Bolton, and a Swedish striker called Martin Pringle.

Unfortunately, Martin broke his leg against Stockport County in only his second game for us and it ended his career. He had already suffered a bad injury at Charlton and this was another nasty one. The Stockport player who fouled him, a long throw specialist called Dave Challinor, only got a yellow card for it but Carlton Palmer, who was his manager at Stockport at the time, fined him afterwards which gives you an idea of how bad a challenge it was.

Andy Todd was immense, the best centre-half I have ever played with. He refused to wear long sleeves, he just didn't like them, always preferred short sleeves. So whenever he got given long-sleeved shirts, Andy would cut them down to size with scissors. The kitman used to go mental at him, 'That'll come out of your wages! They're £40, those shirts!'

He was a quiet lad but we all knew he had a hard streak in him because he had dished out a fair bit of treatment on the pitch in his time. After he left us he went on to Blackburn where he played in the Premier League for quite a few seasons and won their player of the year award, which didn't surprise any of us.

Andy was a special player, he never seemed to need to put his head through the ball when he was defending although he did when he was in the opposition box. In fact he scored a few crucial goals for us that helped us avoid relegation. Andy was so composed, he would calm us down and get us passing. We had a run of really tough games as we were coming to the end of the season and still weren't safe from the drop but Andy scored a great header at Molineux to beat Wolves 1–0. Those were three vital points that really helped us stay up.

When Grovesy told us he was taking us back to Malmo again that summer, we all thought, 'Happy days! Bring out the cigars!' But he was still a player too and he was wise to the sort of thing that we might get up to. So right at the start of the trip he gathered a few of the senior players together and told us, 'I'm not going to treat you like kids, you older lads. Make sure the younger players get sent back to the hotel and you can stay out for a couple of drinks as long as you don't go mad.'

Unfortunately that was like a red rag to a bull for Gally – he loved the idea of being given permission to go out drinking.

He dragged us straight down to the nearest nightclub even though we had a game the following day. It was just our luck that Grovesy and his assistant manager Graham Rodger walked into exactly the same place we had chosen. But if Graham looked furious when he saw me that was nothing compared to the shock on Grovesy's face when he spotted Gally swinging round a pole dancer's pole with a cigarette and a beer.

Right on cue Livvo turned up back from the bar with another round of beers. Quick as a flash he tried smoothing things over: 'Alright Grovesy? Look, I've got you a beer.' 'Thanks lads, don't mind if I do,' said Grovesy. 'Now I think you'd all better make yourselves scarce, don't you?'

As it turned out, the manager left before us and we stayed there all night. But that came back to haunt us the next day because we had a game to play. Graham Rodger shook his head at us before we kicked off, 'You're a disgrace, you lot, you all stink of booze. We've got to try to put on a good performance today because there's going to be a decent crowd.'

Generally everyone got 45 minutes or so in friendlies like that but at half-time Graham pointed to me and Gally and said one of us would have to play the full game because of the numbers we had available.

Before he had a chance to say anything, I quickly jumped in with, 'Well, it'll have to be you, Gally, because I drank much more than you.'

I had walked off before poor old Gally had even had a chance to get his words out. In the second half he was really beginning to struggle because he was in no real state to play. He was even being sick but the only way he managed to persuade the managers he should come off in the end was because of so-called blisters. I couldn't see anything wrong with his feet!

Despite the state we were in, we actually did alright for an hour in that match but then we fell apart in the last 20 minutes when the after-effects of our drinking kicked in and lost quite badly in the end.

Scandinavia is an amazing place, the best place I have visited I think. We were absolutely gobsmacked by how stunning the women were – I know it's a cliche but when we first arrived we found ourselves pointing out one incredible-looking woman after another. In fact, by the end of our first visit we got bored of doing it because after a while we had got used to how gorgeous everyone looked, it wasn't out of the ordinary any more. Even the blokes looked beautiful; in fact half of them were better-looking than the women.

They loved cycling as well, the Swedes. We were in a club once and some people asked us if we wanted a lift back to our hotel as they were heading that way. We said yes but when they turned up to pick us up, they were on bikes. We couldn't believe they were being serious but we ended up straddling the back of these four bikes balanced precariously right over the back tyre with our legs going all over the place. I hadn't done that since I was a kid!

# 15

# Paying Peanuts

Paul Groves had put together a management team around him who would immediately earn the respect of the fans and the players. He had been our skipper and was now player-manager for starters. He had another popular former player, Graham Rodger, as his assistant manager and he also had Paul Wilkinson, who was a bit of a Grimsby legend, as his first team coach. Wilko was brilliant, a really good coach who had done his UEFA B Licence on the same course as me. We had massive respect for Grovesy but it was hard for him and 2002/03 turned out to be a tough season for Grimsby Town.

The writing was on the wall before a ball was even kicked because although Paul was already working with a tight budget when he first started the job, he was then told he would have even less money for his first full season in charge. We knew we were going to be up against it because the ITV Digital cash had gone and we couldn't afford to bring any decent new players in. We put on a show and gave it our best shot but I knew deep down we were in trouble that season.

It is perfectly understandable that those in charge didn't want to put the future of the club in jeopardy because this was a period of great financial uncertainty for foot-ball, with clubs like Bradford City and Leicester going into administration. But it was frustrating as a player as we all wanted to have a proper crack at staying in that division.

Grovesy was quite like Lennie in that he was very interested in the scientific approach to the game. He was getting towards the end of his playing days so when he was given the Grimsby job this was his chance to make his mark in management. But his problem that season was that the players he had just weren't good enough. That is why we got relegated – in fact we finished bottom of the league, the only time that happened in my career.

He was let down by the players but the board showed faith in Grovesy and kept him on for the 2003/04 season. The problem with dropping down to the third tier, which was still called the Second Division in those days, was that the revenue coming into the club was going to go down so Grovesy's budget certainly wasn't going to get any better.

I had previously suffered back-to-back relegations under Mick Lyons and Bobby Roberts when I was just starting out in my career and I could really sense the same sort of feeling this time that we were on a downward spiral. Players were coming into the dressing room at the start of the 2003/04 season with the wrong attitude. They thought we would go straight back up because we had gone down a division and we would be playing lesser sides – but as far as I was concerned we had lost some players and were worse than the season before. Once you're on that slippery slope, it's almost like losing becomes a habit that is hard to break out of. We did bring some new players in but we were paying peanuts – and you know what happens if you pay peanuts.

I was settled at the club but that summer of 2003 was really the start of my downfall at Grimsby. We had been relegated and my first reaction was that, as one of the players, I felt my share of the blame. I wanted to be loyal to the club because I was part of the squad that suffered relegation and I wanted to put things right the following season. But you can't put things right on your own.

I think the fans always knew that, whatever league I was playing in, I would always set my own standard which had to be met. Yes, I would have the occasional bad game but it did hurt me when I played poorly and I think sometimes with some players it doesn't hurt enough. Now that I'm on the other side of the fence in management, I can understand that much better – it sometimes hurts the manager more than it does the players when you lose and you can't let that happen.

But regardless of how keen I was to put things right at Grimsby, the reality was that I was out of contract. And it was at that stage that Hull City made it known they were keen on signing me. Grovesy was happy for me to have a new contract at Grimsby even though I was 34 but I couldn't ignore the interest from Hull, especially as they were just moving into their big new stadium. It all made sense because I was sorting out a few things in my personal life and it seemed to be a good idea for me to move on from Blundell Park and start afresh.

It was a win-win situation from my point of view because I didn't want to move too far away from the area and Hull was just a stone's throw away. I felt at that point that Grimsby had had the best of me, we had just got relegated and Grovesy would probably relish the chance to bring in some new people. Hull were offering me exactly the same sort of money that I was already on and even though they were a league lower than Grimsby they had this brand new ground and were clearly on the up with the potential to pull in big crowds. My thinking was that it might be the last chance in my career to play in front of 20,000, so why not?

The fact that they had recently appointed Peter Taylor as manager was another aspect that appealed to me because he had huge managerial experience – he had even been caretaker manager of England and given David Beckham the captaincy for the first time. I was already thinking ahead to what I might do after retiring from playing and I thought I might learn something from Peter that might help me if I moved into coaching and management.

I have massive respect for Grovesy so when Hull made their approach, I was totally open with him and told him I was going to go over to Hull to speak to them. He was fine with it and just asked me to keep him in touch with how things were going. I did just that and there were never any problems between me and Paul Groves – during that whole period when I was negotiating with Hull City, we were totally open with each other, I kept him up to date with what was happening and I made it clear that if the Hull deal fell through I wasn't interested in going anywhere else. Paul said he was happy to have me back if things didn't work out. I rang him pretty much every day because I wanted to be fair to him as he obviously needed to know what new players he might need to bring in.

I spoke to Peter Taylor and he was keen to have me. We agreed verbally what the deal would be – Hull were offering me exactly the same money that I was being offered at Blundell Park so if anyone tries to tell you that I was interested in leaving for more money, that's just not true. Peter said to me, 'Look, John, you're not going to shaft us now, are you? I don't want you going off getting your agent to go talking to other clubs and using us as a bargaining tool to get a better offer somewhere else.'

But I told him I didn't have an agent as such, just a guy who was acting on my behalf. And I gave him my word that I wouldn't talk to any other clubs. Altogether, Peter was looking to bring in three players at the same time – as well as me there was Michael Dawson's brother Andy from Scunthorpe and Richard Hinds from Tranmere.

Everything seemed to be agreed so shortly afterwards I found myself going over to Hull to meet their people and sign the contract. I had checked into a hotel and had my suit on ready to do business when I got a phone call, 'John, it's bad news.'

At first I thought someone's car had broken down and the meeting was off. But it was much worse than that. 'Sorry, but your deal's off. The other two deals are still going ahead – Andy Dawson and Richard Hinds – but they're taking a young right-back called Alton Thelwell instead of you. He's been released by Tottenham and they've gone for him instead.'

I was flabbergasted. I said, 'Is this a wind-up or what? I've just spoken to the secretary at Hull City who was asking me for my National Insurance number.'

As far as I was concerned, everything had been agreed and just needed to be signed and sealed. But it soon became clear that this was no wind-up – the deal had fallen through at the last minute. I was told Peter Taylor hadn't phoned me personally to break the news because he was so embarrassed by the way it had been handled.

I was even out of pocket, having spent my own money on booking into a hotel for nothing – but that wasn't what I was upset about, I just wanted a phone call from the club giving a proper explanation. I understand that a manager is wheeling and dealing to get the best squad he can and if he can get a better player in, he will do. There is no room for sentiment and I'm on the other side of the fence now so I know what happens – but there's a proper way of doing things.

Peter Taylor did ring me later on. He said, 'John, you can call me every name under the sun and I deserve it.' I replied, 'Peter, I've got more respect for you than that. But my problem is, what do I tell Grimsby Town now? They might tell me they've already signed a replacement for me and then I won't have a club to go to at all.'

I rang Grovesy and, true to his word, he was happy for me to come back to Grimsby on the same terms that we had discussed before. But before I had the chance to arrange to go in to the club and sign the contract, he rang me back with another bombshell.

'Macca, you know that deal we talked about? I'm afraid the club say you can't have it now. If you want to come back to Grimsby, you'll have to take a drop of £800,' he said.

It seemed to me that they wanted to give me a slap on the wrist for having nearly moved to Hull City and I was in no position to do anything other than to accept the lower offer.

The thing that seemed to annoy the chairman John Fenty most was the idea that I was keen on going to Hull because I felt they had ambition. He seemed to think that I was implying Grimsby didn't have any ambition, which wasn't the case at all. The appeal of going to Hull had many different aspects.

Grovesy told me that he had explained to the chairman that it wasn't about money, which was true. But I had never said anything about Grimsby lacking ambition – it was a combination of different things that led me to Hull City. But this idea that Grimsby somehow lacked ambition seemed to really rankle.

I think Grovesy was trying to box clever and thought that by talking about Hull's ambition, it might spark the chairman into finding a bit more in the budget for me – but it well and truly backfired.

If I had signed three weeks earlier, I could have got an extra £800. It was a smack in the face for me but you could argue that I deserved it for nearly going to Hull and turning my back on Grimsby. From that point of view, you can't blame Grimsby for doing what they did.

But every year after that, the money on offer to me seemed to get worse and worse. True, the team finished low down in the league several seasons in a row so you might say that's fair enough – if you get relegated, you can hardly expect a pay rise. It is like any job, if you do it badly you'll pay the price.

I rang Paul after he too was sacked and told him the players had let him down, including me. I was disheartened at that point and I was just about ready to pack it in – I was in my mid-30s and I was pretty much paying the club to play. I certainly wasn't doing it for the money.

In football, experience as a player counts for something for a few years but when you get to a certain age, there are people in charge who want to cut your salary right back just because you're older. It's no use telling them that you're doing just as good a job as you were when you were 21 – to them, you're almost a liability rather than an asset.

I am a great believer that appearances should count for much more when it comes to what you get paid as a footballer. In other words, if you are in your 30s but you are still worth your place in the side and keep getting picked week in, week out, that should be reflected in your wages. Instead, it's usually based on your market value, which means when you get older you're not a long term prospect so you're not worth much. What used to really grate with me was the 21-year-old kids we had at Grimsby who would get paid more than me but were sitting in the stands most weeks.

# 16

# Bursting The Boil

When Grovesy got the sack, they brought in Nicky Law. It was already March, we were struggling against back-to-back relegations and his appointment seemed to be the last throw of the dice. I didn't know him from Adam, other than that he had done a decent job at Chesterfield.

I was sitting with our goalkeeper Aidan Davison when we heard Nicky had been appointed. Aidy's phone started buzzing and it was one of the lads he still knew from his Bradford City days ringing to tell him Nicky Law had got the Grimsby job. Aidy immediately put his phone down and said, 'Right, I'm off to see the chairman. I'm not playing under him.'

Aidy had been at Bradford with Nicky and hadn't been impressed with him when he was there. He had now been brought in at Grimsby seemingly as a stop-gap at first to try to keep the club up and on the basis that he would stay on after that if he succeeded. But Aidy said he wouldn't play for him, he would develop a mystery calf injury if need be.

It seemed like Nicky was quite unpopular with quite a few people but I couldn't say I didn't like him – I have always had respect for every manager I have played for, whether I thought they were good, bad or indifferent. I hardly spoke to him at first because when he arrived I was out injured with a hernia and wasn't playing but there seemed to be some kind of rift between us right from the off. I didn't fall out with him as such but as we approached the crucial final few games at the end of the season, I certainly didn't agree with him about the way he was preparing the team.

In the end, it all came down to a do-or-die last match of the season away at Tranmere. Even though I probably wasn't 100 per cent fit, I thought I had got myself fit enough to play and I was desperate to be part of that game. It was a huge match because survival was still in our hands and we knew we would have a big away support following us.

But Nicky didn't want me to play, 'No, we'll leave you until next season. Get yourself right.' I was upset because I thought I knew better than him. Players always do think they know more than their manager.

We had signed a smashing lad on loan called Paul Warhurst, who had quite a successful career with Sheffield Wednesday and Bolton. He was a great lad, as quiet as a mouse and very polite. He would come in to the club, quietly sort out his kit, barely speak to anyone and at the end of a game, away he went again. Before the Tranmere game we had a big team meeting at the hotel – but there was no sign of Paul.

We all wondered where he was – but when we got to the ground, there he was in the dressing room, already changed into his warm-up kit. I couldn't understand why he wasn't at the team meeting for such an important game for the club. There is a way of doing things the right way and this didn't seem right. We needed to prepare properly for this game and yet here we all were asking ourselves why Paul was meeting us at the ground rather than in the hotel. Maybe he lived over there, but I didn't care. I wanted everything done right and that was something else where I took issue with how Nicky Law was handling things.

Grimsby did take a massive number of away fans to the game and there was a big crowd at Prenton Park, over 10,000. Chesterfield, who were the other team in the relegation battle, were playing Luton and when Darren Mansaram scored to give us a 1–0 lead over Tranmere it looked like we were going to be safe, whatever Chesterfield did. We were playing well and everyone was buzzing.

But rather than going for a killer second goal, Nicky sent out the message for our players to stop bombing forward and keep things tight. I suppose it seemed fair enough to try to hang on to what we had at that point because we had started the day two points ahead of Chesterfield. We knew they were still 0–0 against Luton so that meant even a draw would have been enough for us to survive.

We thought we were staying up at this point and the Grimsby fans were in full voice. But trying to shut up shop changed the momentum of the game and gave Tranmere more of an incentive to come and attack us. Suddenly they started to get some joy coming forward and they looked dangerous in front of goal, particularly a little striker called Iain Hume who was very decent in the air.

Hume equalised for Tranmere with a header but they then had a man sent off almost immediately afterwards which gave us encouragement again. Even with ten men, though, they scored again to go 2–1 ahead and by this stage we just didn't look like getting back into the game. Even a defeat wasn't necessarily going to send us down as long as Chesterfield didn't win and the last we had heard, they were still goalless with Luton. But as we got back into the dressing room we heard that typically Chesterfield had scored with 2 minutes to go. They were safe and Grimsby had been relegated again.

I was fuming. It really hurt me, particularly for the fans who had paid big money throughout the season to support us. After all the years I had played for Grimsby I really felt this club was my club and it hit home harder for me than anyone else in our dressing room, I think. I may have been born in Middlesbrough but this was my home now. I lived there and I was going to stay living there after I had packed in playing. It was a far cry from the players who had been brought in on short-term loans and would be off on their travels somewhere else again the following season.

After the game, Nicky told the players, 'I honestly thought Chesterfield were going to get beat today.' I just looked at Dave Moore and shook my head. It was all I could do not to get up and just walk out because he had totally misjudged the situation as far as I was concerned.

Since then, I have never seen eye to eye with Nicky Law and I don't really know why because I have never said a bad word about him. He must have been upset that he didn't get kept on by Grimsby after the relegation following that Tranmere defeat – but that was hardly my fault. He didn't get the job because we got relegated, it's as simple as that. I have come across Nicky a few times since because we have both been working in non-league – me at Harrogate and him at Alfreton – so we have shaken hands but that's about it.

• • •

I didn't shed any tears when Nicky Law left but I'll be honest, I was very sceptical when Russell Slade was appointed manager in the summer of 2004 as his replacement. And I wasn't the only one. His last job had been at Scarborough, who had finished a not-very-impressive fifteenth in the Conference the previous season. The players all thought, 'A non-league manager? Here we go. He'll drag us even further down.'

But even though this was Russ's first permanent job as a manager of a Football League club, when we started to find out more about him we discovered he had actually had a couple of spells as caretaker manager at Notts County and Sheffield United. He had never been a professional footballer but trained as a school teacher and although Scarborough had struggled in the Conference the previous season, they had a fantastic FA Cup run under Russ and only got knocked out 1–0 by Chelsea in the fourth round.

And before Russ actually arrived at the club, I started to hear some really good things about him from other players who had worked with him. Jamie Forrester, who had a couple of spells at Grimsby, told me, 'You'll love him, Macca, he's brilliant. He's so bubbly, you'll love playing for him.'

Maybe we shouldn't have been so quick to judge Russ because I had actually had the same doubts about Alan Buckley because of his non-league background when he first came to Grimsby – and look how wrong I was about him!

When Russ came to the club to meet everyone, Jamie was right – he was a big character with a big, bald head and I liked him straight away. And one of the first things he did was to show respect for the senior players, which was important because he was going to need them on board to lift the dressing room after back-to-back relegations.

One of the first things he said to us was that he didn't want the first team and the reserves to be separate, he wanted us all in it together. In the first week of pre-season training he set up a competition to play in the afternoons that was like a football version of the TV show *It's a Knockout*. The games he devised were all based on ball skills and at the end of the week the winners got little prizes like Mars bars. It was great, we all enjoyed it so much.

Russ brought in a few of the younger lads at the club, some fresh faces and some of the seniors who had been around the club for a while and mixed us all up into groups for these *It's a Knockout* games. He used that as a way of bringing the club back together after the disappointment of those two relegations. For me, it was just like going back in time twenty years to when Alan Buckley arrived. His methods were exactly the same and he brought us all together just like Alan did.

He quickly won the respect of the senior lads, people like me who had been around for a while, and newcomers like Justin Whittle who had been signed from Hull. Russ liked to call us over and consult with us over things, which felt fantastic. It was good to feel valued. Russ's enthusiasm was infectious and because he had been trained as a school teacher, he was great at communicating his ideas.

He seemed to win the fans over and although we didn't have that much success on the pitch in his first season, he quickly made an impact on the way we played. Some might describe it as a long ball, but I think it was just more direct than we had played in the past and we had plenty of runners, people like Michael Reddy from Sunderland. One of the things with Russ was that he never tried to fit square pegs into round holes.

Funnily enough, Russ didn't play me very much to start with. I think he followed the advice of Graham Rodger who felt that Jason Crowe was a better bet than me because he had younger legs. Between them they thought I was coming to the back end of my career and for a while during pre-season it looked like I was completely out of the picture.

I was on the bench for the first league match away at Darlington and didn't come on but I felt as fit as I had done for ten years. I was raring to go because the doom and gloom had all gone and this guy was giving me a real injection of enthusiasm. As a right-back, it can be frustrating when you're on the bench because you know there's very little chance of you coming on unless there's an injury to a defender. If you're losing, you're not a game-changing player that the manager is going to throw on to get an equaliser and if you're winning, the manager probably isn't going to change the team either.

It is not like being a striker on the bench when you always think you have got a chance of coming on as a tactical change. But under Russ being a substitute didn't affect me at all. I was enjoying training because of Russ's enthusiasm – and my positive attitude seemed to rub off on him too. He used to go round saying to the other lads, 'Look at Macca, he lifts me. When I'm down because we've been beaten, he lifts me because of his attitude. That's how I want it, the way he does it.'

In the second league game of the 2004/05 season at home to Boston United, he gave me my chance and after that I was a regular in the team. The only snag was that Russ had decided to go with wing-backs. So here I was, at the age of 35 and in the twilight of my career, expected to bomb up and down like I was ten years younger!

But I loved it of course – we played with three centre-backs so here was my chance to get forward almost as much as I liked and get some shots on goal. I didn't have to defend all the time and it really suited my style. I didn't score too many goals in my career but I did get a couple that year which qualifies as quite a prolific season for me. We had a player signed from Millwall called Ronnie Bull who would often play wing-back on the left. He was a good footballer and a funny guy but he didn't really have the legs even though he was years younger than me.

As a wing-back I suppose it must have been much harder work because you had to do so much more running but it seemed easy for me. I was buzzing because I felt fitter and sharper than I had for ages – it felt like being a young kid again. That formation suited me as a player, there was less pressure on me as a defender generally because of my role in the team and also probably less expectation on me personally. Here I was at 35 playing wing-back – what do you want from me?

When it came to the 2005 player of the year awards ceremony, I won virtually a clean sweep. I got the official player of the year award and various supporters' awards – seven in all. It was a very exciting night for me because although I had won the young player of the year award before, I had never won the main player of the year award. It seemed to be a fair reflection of just how much I had enjoyed the season and how much my game had flourished under Russ.

I was out of contract that summer but with a sackful of awards, I was pretty confident that I would be able to get a decent deal for the following season. We hadn't got anywhere near the play-offs but we had had a steady season and stopped the rot, which was the most important thing – and I had got on with the manager brilliantly so things seemed very positive as far as I was concerned.

But things didn't exactly work out how I expected when I met Russ to see what the club were offering me. He pushed over a piece of paper to me with a figure on it and I just looked at him in disbelief.

'I hope that's just appearance money. Is that just a bonus you're talking about? You've got to be kidding, that can't be what you're offering me as my wages,' I said.

But Russ shook his head, 'Sorry, that's your contract.'

It was £300 a week. I had just won a virtual complete sweep of the player of the year awards and had one of my best ever seasons. I was the club's longest-serving player, I had played thirty-nine league games that season and yet here they were trying to make me one of the lowest-paid players on their books.

The thing is that no one could pull the wool over my eyes because Russ had been very helpful to me when I first got interested in the management side of football by showing me among other things how to work out your budget for players' wages. The system he explained to me was one where you had a handful of players right at the top of the list, maybe including a couple of valuable strikers who you would need to pay really good money. Then there would be a group of about ten who were your die-hards, the lads who would be in the first team most weeks if they were fit – they would also need to be on quite good money. And the third group would be on the least money – your squad players who were on the fringe, with the young lads right at the bottom.

I could see on his budget sheet that he had on his desk in front of him that I was right down near the very bottom of the list. There was a young first year pro underneath me and that was about it. Russ said to me, 'The word's come from the top – Let's burst the boil.'

So was I a boil that needed lancing? I had no idea what the club were trying to do to me – was someone trying to get rid of me? It seemed to me like they were offering an insulting amount of money so I would walk away.

I said to him, 'Russ, I can't play for that sort of money. I have bills to pay – it would cost me nearly my whole wages in petrol money driving over from where I live. I'd have to retire rather than play for that. I can't live on that, I've got four kids.'

On top of your basic weekly wages, you would get appearance money and a win bonus as well but those were only small amounts and of course everyone else got that as well so it didn't alter the fact I would be something like the fourth worst paid player in the squad.

Don't get me wrong, I wasn't getting big-headed and asking for silly money just because I had won a few player of the year awards. All I wanted was the same as I had been on before, which was £650 a week, although I had been hoping they might push me back up to £800 in recognition of how well I had done the previous season. But instead, they cut it by over half – just because they knew I was getting older and didn't have much of a long-term future left.

The manager tried his best to help me out by seeing if he could make up my wages to something more like what I was already on by adding in some extra for coaching duties. I was already doing the School of Excellence and getting an extra £50 a week for that. Deep down I still felt hurt that they weren't offering me at least the same as I had been getting before and paying me extra on top of that for the additional coaching, but I didn't really feel I had any choice so I told Russ I was happy to do more coaching because I was keen to move into that area anyway.

We went over to speak to the vice-chairman Peter Furneaux and Russ explained all the coaching duties he wanted me to do. The things he had in mind were the first team preparation in the mornings, warm-ups, cool-downs and ball work, that kind of thing, before Russ took over, which was fine by me. Russ did a good job of selling this idea, Peter made a note of it all and said he'd consult with the chairman and let me know.

I got a phone call not long afterwards from the chairman John Fenty, who said he wanted to run through the extra duties I needed to do. As well as all the things Russ had talked about, the chairman also wanted me to go and scout at least one game a week, plus he wanted me to carry on doing the School of Excellence two nights a week and on Sundays as well. And this was on top of being a full-time player!

I said, 'How will I be able to fit all that in? I'll never be at home!' But John replied, 'I thought you'd be pleased to get out of the house, you've got four kids, haven't you?'

I told him I actually liked spending time with my family and I didn't see enough of my kids as it was. I was beginning to lose it – but it got worse. When I asked him how much I would get paid for all this extra work, he said it would be £50. That was how much I was already getting for doing the School of Excellence for Neil Woods! I said it was no deal, I would just carry on as I was. But the chairman said that wasn't an option – I either had to do all the coaching duties he wanted me to do for £50 or none at all. It was take it or leave it.

As a result of that, I stopped doing the School of Excellence, which was a great shame for everyone because they were getting a good coach for only £50 a week.

That still left me with the offer of a contract for only £300 a week. I did the sums but after tax I worked out I just couldn't sign for as little as that. I told Russ and he advised me to set up a meeting with the chairman. I had no axe to grind with him – I just wanted an explanation as to why he could justify dropping the wages of a multiple player of the year award-winner from £650 to £300.

We met at what was still known then as the Inn on the Park and his explanation was simply, 'You're getting older. There are players in the squad who are getting more than you because they've got potential.'

In the end I managed to get it up to £400 with a bit of help from Russ but it was still a disgrace. Financially it made no sense for me to carry on at Grimsby but I did anyway. Basically in those last two seasons I played for the fans and for myself because I loved the club.

I didn't realise at the time, but if I had left Grimsby at that stage and played non-league football I could have been a lot better off financially. There is some very good money paid at the top level of non-league football these days and of course if you're semi-professional you can get a job as well.

What upset me was that, yes, I was 36 and not getting any younger, but I should have been paid what I was worth according to my performances on the pitch, not based on how old I was. Not all right-backs are the same, just as not all fish filleters are the same. If you pay £650 for a fish filleter, you'll get a better one than if you only pay £300. And without blowing my own trumpet, Grimsby would never be able to get someone to replace me as right-back for only £300 a week. All I wanted was value for money – pay me for what I have done, not what you think I might be capable of doing in the future.

Why was I treated like that? I don't know for sure but my best guess is that some people at the club got upset about my possible move to Hull City in 2003 – I can't think of anything else that might have caused it. I haven't run over the chairman's cat or done anything else to offend him as far as I know. I have tried to smooth things over with him but it still rankles and it does leave a sour taste in my mouth.

When John Fenty gave me an interview for the manager's job later on I had hoped things might have changed and his opinion of me might have mellowed – but I didn't get the job so now I'm resigned to the fact that I might never be given an opportunity to prove myself as a manager at Blundell Park.

It is a crying shame because after all the years of service that I gave to the club as a player, you would normally expect to be given a helping hand on the managerial ladder – that's how it always used to happen at the club. When Bill Carr was chairman, ex-players who were keen to move into management always seemed to be given a chance. They would start maybe with the youth team and then get the assistant manager's job and even the manager's job – it happened with people like Richard O'Kelly, Ian Knight, John Cockerill and Paul Groves.

But when it came to me, the club's record appearance holder, it was a case of, 'See ya.' Not even kit man.

Some people might say it was maybe just that the club thought I wasn't good enough or experienced enough at that stage – everyone is entitled to their own opinion but I think they're wrong. Just look at the club's overall record over the last few seasons – Grimsby have mainly been on a downward spiral. I defy anyone to say that most of the managers they have appointed recently have done better than I could have done.

I would never have any ill feelings towards Grimsby Town because I love the club, I really do. If they can get it right and get all the way back up to where they belong, that would be brilliant. There would be no one more pleased than me because it pained me to see them get relegated down into non-league. The fans have always been brilliant with me and I wouldn't want their club – because it is their club, much more so than whoever happens to be the chairman at any given time – dragged through the mire.

I have got nothing personal against John Fenty but I was disappointed about what happened. Lots of people get a start in management and then it's up to you what you make of it – 99 per cent of players who are at a club for more than ten years get given that start so I did feel angry that I didn't get it.

Alan Buckley told me later he wanted me to help him out when he took over as manager for a third time and Stuart Watkiss also told me he wanted me when he got the care-taker job – but I didn't get approached on either occasion.

# 17

# The Final Curtain

I managed to put all the upheaval over my contract behind me and get myself ready for the 2005/06 season – my twentieth campaign as a Grimsby Town first team player.

Early on in that season we pulled off a memorable giant-killing act. Playing big teams in cup competitions when you're at a smaller club like Grimsby can be a bit of an eye-opener – the attitude of the big-name players isn't always what you expect. It had really surprised me when we drew Tottenham at home in the League Cup in 1991 and found ourselves up against Gary Lineker. He has the image of being an all-round Mr Nice Guy but he came across as being very arrogant when he played at Blundell Park and wasn't very complimentary about our ground.

We lost that game 3–0 but I have much happier memories of our later League Cup tie against Spurs in September 2005 when we beat them 1–0 thanks to a last-minute goal by Jean-Paul Kalala. It so happened it was my 700th game in all competitions and the chairman John Fenty presented me beforehand with a commemorative cutlery set and also a special shirt with '700' on the back. We weren't necessarily the best of mates but there he was raising my arm up in the air to get cheers from the crowd. It was nice what he did that night, I'll give him his due.

To top it off, we played really well. We had worked hard on our tactics all week. Our game plan was to keep Tottenham in front of us, not let them come through the middle but force them to try to go round the outside. We were in League 2 under Russell Slade that season and Spurs put out a pretty strong side so we were real underdogs. Paul Robinson was in goal for Spurs and they had players like Ledley King, Michael Carrick, Jermain Defoe, Robbie Keane and Aaron Lennon in their side.

I was up against Andy Reid, who was a quality player but I felt I had the edge over him in terms of pace even though I was coming up towards my 37th birthday. Not only did I think he wouldn't get past me but I thought I could get him running back the other way. I enjoyed that game, we got a few breaks and when Kalala smashed in his thunderbolt of a volley so late on we just knew there was no way back for Spurs.

Robbie Keane came up to me afterwards and said congratulations – he knew my name which was a nice touch because you wouldn't necessarily expect a top pro like him to have heard of someone like me. I asked him if I could swap shirts but he said they had all been told they weren't allowed to give their shirts to us because they had promised to give them to the club to be auctioned. That was a real shame.

The same thing happened in the next round when we played Newcastle. I think I have only kept one opposing player's shirt from my whole career and that was Bryan Hughes's Charlton top from when we played them in the League Cup. When you're on a high after some of these really big games, getting a shirt as a souvenir isn't necessarily the first thing on your mind.

I also used to wonder whether the other team would all be thinking, 'What on earth do I want a Grimsby Town shirt for?' And that's not to mention the fact that I would be charged £45 for giving my shirt away. It was hard enough keeping your own Wembley ones!

The game against Newcastle after we had beaten Spurs was really tough. It was at Blundell Park again but they were a really decent side with the likes of Scott Parker and Alan Shearer playing. I was marking Charles N'Zogbia, who was quick but he never really managed to out-pace me. I don't know what it was but that season I felt as sharp as I had done when I was playing two divisions higher.

It was more or less a backs-to-the-wall job with us defending and trying to keep Newcastle out for most of the game. It looked like we might hang on for a draw but towards the end of the game Shearer popped up and bang, he scored the winner despite having done very little for most of the rest of the game. That is the sign of a world-class striker – his movement in the box was exceptional.

That was the night that Justin Whittle caught Shearer in the mouth with his elbow as they went up for a header and gave him a couple of stitches. You can still see the scar on his top lip when you see him on *Match of the Day* if you look closely. Justin has told me that he didn't do it deliberately but he certainly seemed to have come off worse in his challenge with Shearer earlier in the game.

Shearer was furious at the time and wanted him sent off but the referee, Mark Halsey, took no action. Then after the final whistle, Justin wanted to shake hands with him but Shearer refused. Justin is one of the nicest men in football and hardly ever raises his voice but I noticed his eyes were glazed over at this point and I think he would have had a fight with him there and then given half a chance.

During the summer, Russ had thrown in the idea of a second testimonial as a bit of an extra sweetener when it came to persuading me to stay. But unlike with my first testimonial, it was just a one-off game second time around rather than a series of events. We approached Peter Taylor because I knew he owed me big time and he had said after the Hull City move fell through that he would try to help me out if I ever needed any favours in the future.

Peter didn't actually come to the game himself but to be fair he did agree straight away to send his Hull City team to play my testimonial, which was in the October of 2005. They had won back-to-back promotions so they were now two divisions above us and because it was a local derby it was quite an attractive-looking fixture. But that still didn't prepare me for what happened.

We were in the dressing room ready to come out onto the pitch but were told, 'You can't come out yet, the kick-off has been delayed.' The fans were still queuing to get in! I was gobsmacked yet again by the magnificent Grimsby fans. Virtually no Hull fans came but the Mariners supporters were out in force so in the end they put some of them in the away end. There were over 5,000 people there that night, which was fantastic. When you look at the kind of crowds we were getting for league matches, you might have only expected 900 or 1,000 for a game of that sort.

I was overwhelmed by how many Grimsby fans turned up on an October night for that game. I have always got on well with the fans but that night was really special. I can't speak highly enough of them.

I had managed to put together something of a 'Legends' side, including quite a few of the old Wembley team but these lads were never going to be able to play a full 90 minutes so the plan had been to give them the second half and play a team of current players in the first half.

I wanted to say a thank you to those current lads as well, especially the ones who had been around for a few years. The problem was that we had a game on the Saturday and Graham Rodger put out a team in the first half that was nearly all reserves. He was playing 3-5-2 with wing-backs against what was virtually Hull's full first team as well so I would like to say I enjoyed the first half but I didn't really – it was very hard work.

After half-time we brought on all the older lads and it was a fantastic trip down memory lane. We had Aidan Davison in goal and loads of other great lads like Jim Dobbin, Alan Pouton, Neil Woods, Paul Futcher, Kev Donovan, Gary Childs, Kingsley Black, Clive Mendonca and Dave Smith. It really was a joy to play with them all together in the same team and although we lost 1–0, it was a real treat for the fans to see such a lot of quality ex-Mariners on the pitch at the same time. Everyone was buzzing by the end of the game – although the problem was that the following weekend we all had to go back to the current team, who were not a patch on what the supporters had seen for 45 minutes at my testimonial.

One or two people such as Ivano Bonetti couldn't make it which was a shame but it was still a wonderful, nostalgic night which gave a glimpse of just how special these players had been for Grimsby Town. A lot of them had retired by now but their awareness was such that they could all still play. Mark Lever turned up without even bringing a pair of boots – he thought he would just be able to borrow a pair out of the boot cupboard that we had at the club. Just before the game started he said to me, 'I only can manage 20 minutes, Macca. Give me a shout after twenty and I'll have to come off.'

I said to him, 'What do you mean? You can do longer than that.' But Mark pointed down at his boots – he had these things on that looked blue bananas! They had ridiculously long studs on them, they were bright blue and bent completely out of shape.

I said, 'Where on earth did you get them from?' Mark explained that the boot cupboard was locked and the only pair he could find were in the kit cupboard, hidden right out of the way at the bottom leaning up against the hot water pipes. They must have been there for ages and had warped completely out of recognition. The leather was all dried out and started to crack if you tried to bend them back into shape.

Poor old Mark, I think they were a size or two too small for him as well so he was in a right mess after 20 minutes. Mind you, having banana-shaped boots gave him the perfect excuse for not being able to kick it straight.

• • •

We had a really good second year under Russell Slade and finished fourth, just outside the automatic promotion places. I was a regular again that season – I played thirty-seven games which as far as I was concerned again proved that the club were wrong to treat me as they had done over the summer.

We had signed a striker called Gary Jones from Tranmere who formed a really useful partnership with Michael Reddy and the pair of them scored over thirty goals for us between them that season. It felt like it was the first time for a number of years that we had reliable strikers who were regularly banging it in the back of the net. We had even been top of the league briefly a couple of times and were still in the automatic promotion places with two games to go. But we drew our last two matches and finished fourth.

We made it to the play-off final after a memorable two-legged semi-final against Lincoln City, who were one of our big rivals. We had been thrashed 5–0 by them in our league game at Sincil Bank only a few weeks before, which wasn't a good sign. But we had finished well above them in the table and when we went back to their place in the first leg we turned the tables on them by beating them 1–0. Unfortunately I injured myself in that game so I missed the second leg and the final.

There was a great crowd of over 8,000 packed into Blundell Park for the second leg and we beat them 2–1. Gary Jones was actually sent off in the last minute so it looked like he would join me on the sidelines for the final but the club appealed against it and the red card got overturned.

The final was held at the Millennium Stadium because the new Wembley was being built and again there was a good turnout of Grimsby fans in the crowd of nearly 30,000. But we played poorly that day, lost to Cheltenham 1–0 and Russell Slade left soon afterwards to go to Yeovil.

Graham Rodger took over from Russ as manager in the summer of 2006 and I was very keen on becoming his assistant. By this stage I was definitely interested in moving over to that side of the fence and my ambition was to become Grimsby Town manager one day – that would have been the pinnacle of my career in lots of ways.

But Graham said he still wanted me to carry on playing and he viewed this as his first big chance in management so he would prefer someone with a bit of experience to help him rather than someone else who was also in their first job in management. Graham had lots of experience as a player and had won the FA Cup with Coventry City against Spurs in 1987 but his only previous managerial experience was when he was briefly caretaker manager after Paul Groves was sacked in 2004. He didn't get the job permanently because they gave it to Nicky Law.

Graham eventually brought in Stuart Watkiss as his assistant, who had previously been manager at Mansfield Town and Kidderminster Harriers. Although I was disappointed not to get the assistant manager's job, I was pleased with the appointment because I liked Stu and I thought he would do a good job. Graham didn't bring him in until the end of July though and he did a lot of the pre-season work on his own which I think he found a tough job.

I will give Grezza his due – he was the only manager other than Lennie Lawrence who got me a pay rise. I wouldn't sign another contract extension on the same money and I was all set to leave that summer of 2006 because I was going to go and do some scouting work for Russ at Yeovil and also had a few offers of some media work. But Graham talked me round and managed to get me an extra £50 a week to stay on for what turned out to be my final season.

Unfortunately for Graham, results didn't go all that well in the first part of 2006/07 and he got the sack by November. I felt sorry for him because I thought he did all right in his short spell – as well as any other manager had done in the previous few seasons. Grezza is a top man and I thought he was hard done by but I'm afraid the fans got impatient because we'd come so close to promotion earlier that year and they didn't want to see us at the wrong end of the table again.

When Stuart got given the caretaker manager's job he asked me to help him out while he was in charge. I was happy to do that of course and he also asked me if I would like to be his assistant if he got the job permanently.

As it was, Stu was only in charge for a few days because the club then brought back Alan Buckley for a third spell as manager. Alan did tell me that he would have liked me as his assistant but the board wanted him to keep on Stu as his number two – so Stu became Alan's assistant and to be fair he did a really good job. Alan was coming back to the club for the first time in six years so maybe didn't have the same bargaining power to get exactly what he wanted that he had a few years earlier.

I had suffered one or two injuries, nothing major, but I was in and out of the side that season and had got disheartened by it all so I told Alan I had decided I was going to finish at Christmas. 'I'm coming up to 38, you can have my contract, I don't even want it paying up, it's hardly worth it,' I told him.

I was starting to feel a bit leggy so I was ready to go. I didn't want to carry on playing to the stage where people thought I was no longer up to it. In the end, I did carry on after Christmas but I had made up my mind I was definitely going to call it a day at the end of the season. It soon got to the point where I was basically just training and not playing. But things changed the week we played Boston United away in February 2007.

I had trained hard all week and felt good. Alan had always praised my training and used me as an example for other lads of how he liked to see his players train. But this week he said to me, 'Macca, I'm going to leave you out this week completely. Spend the weekend at home with the family, there's no point you coming.'

At the time I found this quite hurtful. Gary Croft had been generally playing right-back but he had an injury so I couldn't understand why I wouldn't be in the squad. I reacted defiantly and said to him, 'I tell you what, Alan, I'm not going to stay at home – I will come to the game anyway and watch.' I wasn't quite ready for my pipe and slippers yet.

Crofty had a bit of a ding-dong with Alan before the game because the manager said he was only going to be on the bench because he hadn't trained whereas Crofty thought if he was fit enough to be a sub, he was fit enough to start. As it was, Matt Bloomer played right-back, Gary did start on the bench and we thrashed Boston United at their place 6–0.

It was at that point that I thought to myself, 'You know what, I'm going to get back into that team. I'm not going to let anyone start to pity me or think that my heart's not in it any more.'

The win sparked us onto a decent run of results and after that, I was a regular in the team until the end of the season. But I knew I would be retiring come May.

Having got past the landmark of 750 games, I thought I would finish at home. My last appearance was going to be our final home match of the season against Lincoln City at Blundell Park. It was ideal because it was a local derby, a decent crowd and a good atmosphere.

I had a guard of honour from the other players at the start of the game, which was fantastic. In the end it was a bit of a flat game that ended 0–0 but I got a great reception from everyone in the crowd when I got brought off in the second half.

I gave my boots away because I thought I wouldn't be needing them anymore but I kept my last shirt. Then the gaffer told me, 'Macca, I think we're going to be needing you again next week.' 'What?! I've given my boots away, boss!'

Luckily I had a spare pair so I played again in the last game of the season away at Shrewsbury. An away match like that might have been something of an anti-climax but what I hadn't realised was that it was Shrewsbury's last ever game at Gay Meadow before they moved to their new ground so there was an amazing atmosphere and it was absolutely packed.

It was a good game and I came off again before the end. When they put my number up, everyone stood up and there was a massive round of applause. I turned round because I assumed one of their players was coming off at the same time. But it was for me!

Later on I was chatting to an old guy who was one of the Shrewsbury fans. He came over to me and said: 'I've been coming here for fifty years and I've never ever seen that happen before. You must be someone very special.'

After the final whistle, fair play to the chairman, he took me down and shoved me in front of our fans so it was a nice send-off for me. It was quite emotional because it was then that I finally knew it was over. There was no coming back now.

# 18

# Twelve-Inch Elvis Quiff

My first taste of the management or coaching side of football had come when I was still only in my early twenties. My mate Marcus Newell and I had a look at the local Sunday league scene and thought to ourselves, 'Why don't we put together our own side? We could get some sponsorship, kit them out properly and make a really good job of it.'

We had a head start because pretty much all of our friends were good footballers. Most of them who weren't actually professionals were still getting paid to play a decent level of non-league football on a Saturday. Quite a few of them were playing for Wisbech at that time in the Eastern Counties League.

As Marcus and I were putting together our team, there was another good side around called Freetime Sports who were winning quite a lot of things so we thought we would link up with them. They were regarded as the 'posh' team in many ways because they weren't based at a pub, they were run from a sports shop.

When we met two of the guys who ran Freetime Sports, their secretary sat me and Marcus down and said to us,

OK lads, we've got two teams and yours will be the B team who'll be in the league below the first team. So what we'd love you to try to do is win a cup; that would be fantastic. But there's no need to win the league and get promoted because we've already got a team in the top division.

Marcus and I just looked at each other and then turned to him and said, 'Right, what we'll do is win that league for you.' 'No, no, you don't understand,' he came back at me. 'We don't want you to win the league because then we'd have two teams in the same division and you're not allowed to do that. We'd have to merge into one team. Just stick to winning a cup.'

So I said, 'OK, then, this is what we'll do. We will win our league, we'll get promoted and then you'll have to pack your team in because our team will be better than yours. And we'll win the cup as well, by the way. How's that?'

The secretary didn't like what we were saying at all but the other guy, who was quite a senior police officer, liked our attitude.

So we entered the Grimsby, Cleethorpes and District Sunday Football League and we did pretty much what we had said we would do – we won our league and when we got promoted we only took one player from the other Freetime Sports side because we were better than them. The rest of that group just broke up and went elsewhere.

We had some decent players in our team, people like Jimmy Shaw and Gary Kerr, who was the son of George Kerr, a former Grimsby Town manager who had been in charge before my time at the club. Marcus also played, we had Dave Ellis, a very tidy right-back, a striker called Carl Smaller, and also Jim Harvey who ended up as secretary of the club. Not me, mind you – there was no way I was playing Sunday league myself!

Another good player we had was a midfielder called Paul Goodhand who was very creative and scored plenty of goals, especially from free kicks. I had to go round and get him out of bed as he always used to ring and say he was ill or some other excuse. I would go to his house and get his dad to drag him out of bed.

Goody was one of the best local midfielders I have seen, though, and did have a spell at Blundell Park. He could have made it had he come to Grimsby Town at a different time. He makes the best cup of tea in Grimsby, too. Mind you, he had plenty of practice – one sugar, Goody!

These lads all got paid to play on a Saturday but the amazing thing about them was that none of them went out drinking on a Saturday night, which would be the norm, because we had such a good side playing on the Sunday that they didn't want to be boozed up. That is a phenomenal state of affairs for a Sunday team because normally everyone is either hungover or still leathered from the night before in a lot of Sunday leagues. They weren't having it. 'No, we want to stay sober,' they said.

Some of the other teams in our division were quite good as well – Blossom Way Sports and Jubilee Inn were both strong sides and a lot of the lads who played for Grimsby College also played for Brigg Town on a Saturday. Brigg won the FA Vase in 1996, which is no mean achievement – plenty of professional footballers never win a cup final at Wembley. Another team who were quite handy were called Swigs. They had a group of lads including Ian Cartwright, Ian Stephenson and Stuart Burns, who were all useful players. All in all, there were five or six quite strong sides, which made for a good standard league.

As well as winning that league, we got to the final of the Lincolnshire County Cup for our level, which was a good achievement. In the final we played a team from the south of the county, down near Spalding, who were quite good and had a guy called Graham Drury playing in the centre of midfield who has more recently managed Corby Town and Boston United.

The game was at Boston United's York Street ground which felt like Wembley compared to some of the Sunday league pitches Freetime Sports usually played on. We won the game quite easily because we had a psychological advantage over the opposition even before a ball was kicked by making sure our team were all kitted out properly, with matching tracksuits and bags. When we stepped off the coach looking like a million dollars, you could see our opponents staring at us thinking, 'These must be a great team!'

That level of professionalism had never been done before in our league but after our success, lots of other teams in the Grimsby Sunday League copied us and it caught on. Teams from Grimsby and Cleethorpes hadn't had any success in that county cup for years and years so that was a real feather in our cap to win it.

After a while the standard in the Grimsby League improved all round and before you knew it it, it wasn't really a pub league any more but almost semi-professional. We had a squad of over twenty regulars at Freetime Sports and we played at the police ground, which was a beautiful surface to play on – they even had a groundsman who would be there to greet you, 'Alright, Macca? How's it going? Cup of tea?'

Those were heady days for that league. We changed our name from Freetime Sports to Intersport after a couple of seasons when the shop changed its name – but we kept on winning. We won the league title five times in all and we won the Lincs Cup about five times, including three times in a row, which was unheard of.

Arthur Mann, who was Alan Buckley's assistant manager, played for us quite often as well even though he must have been in his late forties. When he first played, other teams would see he was in the team and think they would run rings round him because they assumed he would be past it – but he was the fittest player of them all. He used to bomb up and down tirelessly and really enjoyed it, so much so that he would ask me if he could play again.

The first time he played, I had forgotten that we used to 'borrow' warm-up tops from Grimsby Town to make us look even more professional. Arthur immediately started asking, 'Where did you get all this kit from, Macca? We've got exactly the same stuff as this back at the club.' I was convinced he was going to stitch me up so when we had to take the gear back and someone started asking where it had been and what had been going on, I tried to get him to help us out by saying, 'Arthur knew all about it. You wore one, didn't you, Arthur?'

But he just denied it all and kept a straight face, 'I don't know what you're on about.' Thanks, Arthur!

Ian Stephenson became a key part of our team but to start with he used to play for our rivals Swigs. I really wanted him to come and join us instead but everyone else said, 'Forget it, you'll never get a Swigs player to come and play for us. It'll never happen.'

But I knew he was a Manchester United fan and I had three tickets for the FA Cup Final so I bribed him with those. I only gave him one, mind you. We all used to get given Cup Final tickets in those days – you would probably get locked up now if you gave them away to someone so he would play for your Sunday league team! I used to joke with Ian that it was the worst deal I ever did, giving away an FA Cup Final ticket like that because he was rubbish. But I was only kidding, he was a good footballer, very fit.

There were some very good footballers playing in that league at the time, quite a few of them should have made it as professionals – Marcus Newell for one, although he was quite successful for various non-league teams like Spalding United, King's Lynn, Wisbech Town and Bedworth United. It was a properly run league, very different to the image that a lot of people have of Sunday league football, with players tearing into each other with bad tackles. We even started to have pre-match meals when we moved to a new base at a pub in Littlefield Lane, it was an impressive little set-up.

We also went on a couple of tours to Amsterdam and Milan and when we were in Italy all the lads went to watch the Milan derby. About eight of us were staying in the same hotel when we were in Milan and I was sharing a room with Marcus and the secretary, a lad called Phil who was a fireman.

Of course, on our very first night, the fire alarm went off in the early hours of the morning. Phil opened the door and all we could see was smoke like a thick fog. I soon learnt that when they say that firemen can be ready in ten seconds flat, they're not kidding – he got dressed as if he was Superman. He was yelling, 'Fire! Quick, everyone out!' But Marcus, being a lazy sod, just lay there muttering, 'It'll be alright. Leave me alone.'

It took him about an hour to finally rouse himself and get up, which was typical Marcus – he was last for everything. Finally we all got ourselves outside and were sitting in our underpants in the middle of the street. Everyone in the hotel had been evacuated as well but somehow we started to get suspicious because it felt like something wasn't quite right. Sure enough, eventually two of our lads sheepishly came down covered in thick white foam as they had tried to set off a fire extinguisher and ended up covered head to toe in the stuff. One of them looked like the Michelin Man. We had only been there a few hours and I was already yelling at them that we were going to get kicked out of the hotel in record time.

When we went to the Milan derby, we had a quiet drink before the match in a bar on the corner right outside the ground and all we could see and hear were police cars and fire engines careering around. The strange thing was we didn't see any actual trouble at all but when we switched on the television later that night there had apparently been mass brawls everywhere and fans setting things alight. There was lots of fighting but we just weren't aware of it at all. It must have been in very specific areas away from where we were.

We didn't think much of Milan, to be honest. We had this idea it was going to be an amazing place but from what we saw of it, it was all high-rise buildings covered in graffiti. We had a really good laugh while we were there but we might as well have been in Leeds.

All the time that Marcus and I were running this side, I was starting to learn about coaching and management. Actually it was quite daunting at first to stand up in front of a group of players – one or two of these lads were older than me as well. When I had to announce for the first time who was playing in the cup final team, I thought I was going to start crying. It was quite emotional letting down some of the lads and I found it quite hard to get my words out. That was a real eye-opener for me.

The pair of us had quite contrasting approaches, which worked quite well, a sort of good cop, bad cop thing. Marcus was maybe the one who tended to let rip a bit more if they had not played well whereas I was more laid back and I would probably be more likely to go round having a quiet word with people. Marcus was much more of a motivator and he's had some success in management.

The skills of being a football manager or coach are broadly the same at any level except in some ways it's harder if you're running a Sunday league side because the players aren't getting paid. It is much more difficult to give them a hard time than a professional who is actually getting paid to play football. Our players weren't getting paid – in fact, quite the opposite, they were paying us. Not that it was always that easy to get them to cough up their subs.

But whatever stick we gave them, these lads took it, because I think they respected me and Marcus and believed in what we were trying to do and the football we were trying to get them to play. We also had a beer together and in quite a few cases we got people's kids involved as well and got a family thing going.

Once I had got a taste for it, I realised this was something I definitely wanted to do in the future. After a few years, I got offered the chance to start coaching with the School of Excellence at Grimsby Town which was a great opportunity for me but it meant I had to knock the Sunday league on the head. I enjoyed working with kids but I missed adult football coaching – that was really where I saw my future after I finished playing.

Apart from anything else, coaching youth teams can be a hair-raising experience at times. We were coming back from a cup match at Lincoln once and the amount of dope being smoked on the coach was unbelievable – the air was so think with it you could hardly see. Then someone said, 'Macca, you realise you could get done as well for passive smoking if they smell it on your hair.'

Quick as a flash, I had my head out of the window and kept it there all the way back from Lincoln. I got such a blow dry, I looked like Elvis by the time we got back. I am not kidding you, I had a quiff about twelve inches high.

They were great lads, they never got into any fights or anything but it all got a bit much sometimes because they were so unpredictable. We had a goalkeeper called Mike Newman, who won us plenty of games but who was also prone to the odd calamity. In one game, the opposition had a hopeful shot at goal from the halfway line and as it went through the air, I looked back at our keeper, whose nickname was Bootsy, and thought, 'Where on earth's he going?' He was shouting, 'It's alright, I'll get it!'

He was running round the back of the goal to retrieve it, thinking somehow it was going miles over the top for a goal kick. But of course it hit the back of the net – and there he was standing the WRONG side of the goal looking like a prize idiot. I wish I'd had a camera to capture that moment – it was hilarious looking back at it now, even though it cost us the game. If it had been on telly, they would never stop showing it on those shows of football's greatest bloopers.

'Are you taking the piss?' I yelled. But Bootsy just said, 'Sorry, lads, I thought it was going over.'

At the School of Excellence, I worked with some very good coaches like Paul Groves and Graham Rodger, who both went on to become managers of Grimsby Town. All that experience has stood me in good stead for later life, including when I got my job coaching at Grimsby Institute's Football Development Centre. You meet players who are noisy on the pitch, the kind of people who are a natural as a skipper and who you might think would be ideal to go into coaching – but then when they stand up in front of a group of players, they can't do it. It is totally different – but

I felt very comfortable with it and enjoyed learning about man-management techniques and how players react.

When I first took up a post at Grimsby Institute, I found it quite easy because it felt like a natural progression. Organising and setting up your team tactically is the most obvious aspect of it – and I think I'm as good as anyone else at that now, without blowing my own trumpet. But the other side of things, managing players, is something that not everyone can do.

# 19

# Frozen Out

Not long after I retired as a player in 2007 I went for the Boston United manager's position but, to be honest, looking back now I wasn't ready for it. When I applied for the job, they had just gone down from the Football League to the Conference – but by the time I had my interview, they had been relegated another division. The club were in financial trouble and had tried to avoid getting a points deduction by doing some wheeling and dealing during their last game of the season when they got relegated – but it backfired and the FA gave them a double relegation.

When that happened, I thought to myself, 'Do I really want this job?' But I went to the interview anyway and the first thing they said to me was, 'John, we've had five managers in here wanting this job and you're the sixth candidate. The five we've seen so far are all good managers, some of them with experience of managing league clubs, with decent budgets, signing good players on good money – and you've not done any of that. Why should we give you the job?'

Lennie Lawrence had given me some advice, which was not to be intimidated, to take command of the situation and really nail any difficult questions you might get thrown at you.

So I thought that's what I would do and my reply was,

They've all been sacked. They've all been at good clubs, they've all had money to spend on decent players – so why aren't they still there then? The reason why they've applied for this job is because they've all been sacked for not getting their previous teams to perform. They've failed whereas I haven't been sacked so how do you know I'm not better than all of them?

But as soon as I answered that question, I started to think I might have gone too far. I bet the Boston United directors all thought, 'He thinks he knows it all, this lad!'

They asked me what players I would be bringing in. When they put the same question to the other candidates, they probably all had proper presentations on flashy projector screens. All I had was an A4 piece of paper to look at. I might as well have written it on the back of a fag packet for how impressive it looked.

I gave them the names of players like Gary Croft and Gary Jones from Grimsby Town, who I knew I would be able to persuade to come with me if I got the job. But the Boston United directors poured cold water on those suggestions and said I would never be able to persuade players like that to go part-time – even though I knew Gary Jones was keen to go part-time. He didn't need the money because he had done really well for himself with some business interests outside the game. He just loved his football and he would play for me because he had told me so. It was the same with Crofty, whose family had their own estate agents business. I also told them I had spoken to the Darlington manager Dave Penney and knew I could get Julian Joachim to come back to Boston again, where he started his career.

They clearly didn't think much of me and gave the job instead to Tommy Taylor, who is a nice guy but got the sack after not much more than a year in charge. Looking back on that interview, I realised I wasn't very good, but at least I hoped I would learn from it for the future.

It was a couple of years before I had my next interview for a manager's job. This time it was Grimsby Town – the one job that you would expect me to be one of the leading contenders for. My name was one of those being linked with the vacancy in all the papers and websites and on the local radio as soon as Mike Newell was sacked by the chairman John Fenty in October 2009.

When I applied for the job, my plan was to have Simon Charlton as my assistant, as I knew him from doing my UEFA A licence coaching badge. He was at Bolton and had all the makings of a really good coach. Simon knew his stuff tactically and he was also strong on the fitness side of things. One of my ideas was to try to bring in a new fitness regime to the club that they had never really seen before. This time, I did a proper presentation and all the directors got a pack each outlining all my plans but the first question I got was: 'Do you see yourself as a manager or assistant manager?'

That threw me a bit straight away. I knew Russell Slade had applied to return as manager and he wanted me to go in with him as his assistant. I had told Russ that I was on the shortlist to be manager and he said he knew that but asked if I would be his assistant if I didn't get the job and he did.

At the time I thought that was good news for me because I had two bites at the cherry. But it was tricky for me at the interview when they asked me whether I wanted to be the manager or the assistant manager. I had to be honest but at the same time I didn't want to upset things with Russell by saying I wouldn't want to be an assistant.

So I put the ball back in their court by asking them, 'Well, what job are you advertising?' And when they said it was the manager's job I told them it was up to them to work out whether they thought I was the right man for that job and then take it from there for the assistant manager's job.

As the interview went on, I started to feel comfortable and thought I knew what I was talking about. Some of the directors praised my presentation and said it was one of the better ones they had seen. By the end of it I was happy that I had convinced the directors that I could do the job and in many ways that was enough for me, whether I was offered the job or not. I think I had shown them that the team didn't need a major overhaul, it needed a bit of tweaking and a different system, with certain players who weren't being utilised properly moving to certain positions. I only felt we would need to bring in one or two new players – it was mainly off the pitch that I felt things needed to be sorted out.

After it was over, John Fenty said he would take me to the door himself and somehow it was at this point that I got the feeling that I wasn't going to get the job.

'Don't be disappointed if you don't get it,' he said, which didn't seem like a hopeful sign. John also told me not to say anything to the local press. That seemed to be something that he had a bit of a bugbear about because he had previously thought I had contacted the papers to promote myself and negotiate contracts in public, which was totally untrue. I would never go out of my way to put across my view in the local newspaper but obviously if one of their reporters comes to you and asks you questions you give them a straight answer.

The board offered the job in the end to the youth team manager Neil Woods, who had been caretaker manager since Newell had gone. In my view they were probably always going to give it to him. I have had a few cross words with John Fenty over the years but I don't bear grudges and I don't think he necessarily has anything personal against me either. What I didn't understand, though, was why they would interview me in the first place if they always intended making Neil Woods manager. Maybe it was a sop to the fans because I had been a popular player and some of them seemingly wanted to see me as manager so he thought he'd at least give me an interview. It felt like the rest of us who were interviewed were just being humoured though, to be honest.

In many ways I was glad Woodsy got the job because I like him and he was someone I had played with. But he had struggled in the month or so that he had been care-taker manager – in fact he couldn't buy a win for ages. He was also looking for an assistant because Newell's number two Brian Stein had also left and I thought I would be tai-lor-made for that role because I had spent my whole career at Blundell Park and knew the club inside out like Neil did.

But instead he brought in Chris Casper to be his assistant – he had been manager at Bury so he had some experience but I didn't think he was the right appointment as he didn't have any feeling for the club or how we liked to play football.

By this time I was working as a coach at Grimsby Institute and it was from my knowledge of the fitness tech-niques they used there that I had formulated a lot of my plans for my application for the Grimsby Town manager's job. So you can imagine I was really cheesed off when I noticed that after Woodsy got the job, a lot of the players from the club suddenly started doing fitness work exactly like I had outlined in the presentation packs I had given to the board at my interview.

I still didn't feel particular bitter about how things had turned out but I was upset when I got overlooked for the youth team job – I wasn't asked even though my credentials for that role were impeccable. I had shown the board I was capable of being first team manager and I had been doing youth team coaching at Grimsby Institute for two and a half years turning out sides who were winning everything in sight.

But I didn't even get asked – instead they gave the job to Robbie Stockdale. Now, I've nothing against Robbie at all, he is a top man. I like him and he is really helpful to us, often sending players our way at the Institute. But I just couldn't understand why I was being frozen out after twenty years at the club. It stank.

I was doing a little bit of consultancy work for the club after I finished playing, nothing major, just helping out with contacts and so on. One of the Grimsby players I was helping out with was Ryan Bennett, who was a promising young player attracting interest from a lot of bigger clubs. I was asked in a radio interview whether I thought Grimsby should sell him – I knew that Peterborough United had been in for him for £500,000 so I said yes, I thought they should sell him.

Grimsby were in League 2, near the bottom of the table and leaking goals for fun – how could you turn down that sort of money in their position? Championship players weren't going for that sort of money, let alone League 2 players. So my opinion was that they should take the money, let the lad move on and do better for himself and then go and buy five Ryan Bennetts. Instead of being near the bottom of the league they could then be near the top.

It made sense to me but the next thing I knew, John Fenty was having a go at me. He was basically saying, 'Why is our most loyal player telling us to sell our best asset?' It made me laugh because they sold him a few weeks later anyway.

Was the chairman still upset by the whole Hull City saga in 2003? Only he knows for sure but he certainly seemed to have wrongly got the impression that I was interested in going to Hull because I felt they had more ambition than Grimsby.

And from that point onwards, things were never really quite the same for me at Blundell Park.

# 20

# Excuse Me But It's His Do

Everyone has a few people in their life they feel really indebted to. I have already mentioned how grateful I am to the families of John Fraser and Marcus Newell. Marcus's mum and dad, Veronica and Dave, were brilliant to me. Those two families really brought me out of myself when I was first at Blundell Park, which was very important for a young lad living away from home. I hardly knew anyone in Grimsby but they got me integrated into the community for the first time. If I had gone back to Middlesbrough with homesickness in those early days, I would never have had the chance to achieve what I did at Grimsby Town so I owe them a great deal.

In addition to them, I owe a huge debt to Lee Stephens. He is a brilliant bloke and he gave me my chance at Grimsby Institute when I finished playing.

Whatever situation you find yourself in, Lee is exactly the sort of guy you want in your corner. Lee really went the extra mile for me when it came to the end of my playing career. I was very keen to get a coaching job at the Institute so in the final few months of my last season, every time I saw him, I would say: 'Alright, Lee. Have you sorted out that job for me yet then?'

As it happened, there was a job vacancy just as I was retiring. I don't remember the exact job description but it was for something like a sports development officer and he said he was going to put in a good word for me. With Lee's help, I thought I was home and dry but at the last minute, it turned out that someone else had already been lined up for it. I thought that meant my chances of working at the institute were over but Lee said, 'Don't worry, leave it with me.'

He went out of his way to speak to the principal and told him,

There's this guy called John McDermott who's coming to the end of the playing career at Grimsby Town. Why don't we bring him into the football academy with Gary Childs, let him help with the coaching and use him as a carrot to bring the kids in? It's an opportunity we can't miss. John's only just finished playing so the kids know exactly who he is. We can use him as PR and get him to go into schools as well.

Lee effectively created a job for me and I'll always be eternally grateful to him for giving me that chance.

One afternoon in 2009 while I was working at the institute, I got a phone call from someone saying it was Gordon Taylor from the PFA. My initial reaction was that it must be a wind-up by one of the lads so I just replied, 'Yeah, yeah, of course it is. Come on, what do you want?'

'No, no, you don't understand, I'm ringing about our annual Merit Award. We give it to a deserving player every year in addition to the main PFA Player of the Year award and Young Player of the Year award,' he said.

By this time I was convinced it sounded like Mark Lever so I just said, 'OK, Big 'Un, you've had your fun, see you later, I've got work to do.'

I hung up but a few minutes later the phone went again and this time it was George Berry, who I knew from his playing days at Wolves and who now worked for the PFA. He said, 'John, I've just had Gordon on the phone. You know he was being serious when he rang you about the PFA Merit Award?'

This time, I did recognise George's voice and realised it wasn't a prank call at all. I apologised and said I thought it was a friend pulling my leg. George said, 'OK, don't worry. I'll get Gordon to ring you again – but this time, don't take the piss, OK?'

When Gordon called again, I explained my mistake to him and he was perfectly understanding. 'It's a massive award,' he told me. 'Jimmy Armfield won it last year and Sir Alex Ferguson the year before that. But we want to give it to you this year because it's such a rare achievement for a player to play for more than twenty seasons for a single club.'

Gordon was right – it is a massive award. The list of people who have won it since it first started in the 1970s is mind-boggling – everyone from the greatest players football has ever seen like Pele, Sir Stanley Matthews and Sir Bobby Charlton to legendary managers such as Sir Matt Busby, Bill Shankly and Brian Clough.

The Merit Award has also been given to unsung heroes from the lower leagues such as long-serving players John Trollope and Graham Alexander and, funnily enough, another Grimsby Town player, Tony Ford.

I was blown away by it. It was hard to imagine me being in such illustrious company. When Gordon started giving me details of the ceremony where I would get the award, the Boro lad in me immediately came out. 'Er, is it free, Gordon?' I piped up.

Of course it was free – this was the annual PFA awards do at the Grosvenor Hotel and it was going to be all expenses paid. I would get my own table for up to ten people for me to invite guests of my choice, they were going to pay for transport down to London and back, accommodation at the Grosvenor and there was an after-show party thrown in for good measure.

It was difficult to decide who to invite seeing as I only had a table for ten and there were so many people who had helped me over the years. The first name on the list was my dad. Strictly speaking, all your guests were supposed to be people who had been involved in your career but there was no way he wasn't coming. My two brothers-in-law came too and I also invited Alan Buckley of course; Lee Stephens, who had given me my break at Grimsby Institute, and Dave Boylen, who had been on my testimonial committee.

I was in two minds whether to invite John Fenty – he was the chairman of Grimsby Town but I had mixed feelings about him. If Bill Carr had still been chairman, there would have been no hesitation. Rightly or wrongly, I didn't invite John in the end but when it came to the actual presentation he made a great speech about me. They had done a video presentation, interviewed me and filmed me at work and playing and they had also gone to the club and spoken to John. To be fair to him, he did say some very nice things about me so I felt a bit guilty about not bringing him along.

It was a great night though, right from the very beginning. I turned up at the Grosvenor with Gary Childs who was sharing a room with me and we couldn't believe the size of the beds for starters – you had to take a running jump to get on them! I had brought along a smart tuxedo to wear but when I went to have a shower just before the actual ceremony, I realised to my horror that the new

shower gel I had brought with me had come open in my bag
– it was a brand new exotic type I had bought that was col-
oured bright burgundy.

That shower gel was absolutely everywhere and I was in
a panic that my shirt and tuxedo were going to be ruined.
I grabbed a brand new white Grosvenor towel to wipe the
bag out – honestly, by the time I had finished, it looked like
someone had slaughtered an animal in there. It was like
there was blood everywhere. But luckily I had packed my
shirt and tuxedo in a separate compartment so they survived unscathed.

There was a huge media preview at the start of the evening with more press there than I had ever seen before. That
was when I met Ryan Giggs and Ashley Young and discovered they had  won the PFA Player of the Year award and
Young Player of the Year awards respectively. Giggsy was a
lovely guy and I had a really good chat with him. He was a
true gent and made me feel important even though he was
the one who was the megastar. The only thing that made my
heart sink was the fact that these two were wearing trendy
silk ties and their own suits whereas I had a penguin suit
and a dicky bow on. I suddenly felt a right tit.

Everyone was sworn to secrecy to keep it hush-hush who
had won the awards until they were actually announced.
After we had all had our photographs taken and media inter-
views done, I went back upstairs and when I found Childsy
I mentioned to him that Ryan Giggs had won the Player of the
Year award. Next thing I knew, I got a phone call from Gary
Jones, who played with us at Grimsby, wanting to know who
had won Young Player of the Year so he could get a bet on!

I told him, 'Gaz, I can't tell you! I'd be hung, drawn and
quartered if I told you and they found out it was me. And
they'd probably take my award away from me.'

I was already enjoying the evening but it got even better when we went into the ceremony itself – our table was right at the front. We had pretty much the best seats in the place, with the Manchester United table behind ours. My heart sank though when they brought the meal out. It was lamb – and that's the only thing I just can't eat. But as soon as Lee Stephens realised, he took charge. He called a waiter over, pointed at me and said, 'Excuse me, but it's his do and he doesn't like lamb.'

Forget about Ryan Giggs, this was my do now apparently! Anyway, Lee sent him off back to the kitchen and the waiter brought me back a big plate of chicken, so I was very grateful to Lee for that.

It was a bit nerve-racking at first when I went up to receive my award because it was live on Sky TV but once I started flowing I felt fine. Jeff Stelling was hosting the awards but he did ask me one question that threw me a bit – he wanted to know if they cut me open, would I smell of fish?

Smell of fish? What was all that about? At least it would have made sense if he had asked if they cut me in half, would I bleed black and white?

It was one of the proudest nights of my life. So many people were saying such nice things to me and people were coming over all night to say well done. Martin O'Neill sat chatting with my dad, who was thrilled because he is a big Celtic fan and Martin had been manager of Celtic only a few years previously. Martin also had plenty of kind words to say about me – he remembered seeing me play when he was at Wycombe.

It was also really touching when the Dutch coach Rene Meulensteen came over from the Manchester United table to congratulate me. He said, 'Well done, you deserve it. But the most important thing of all is you're a nice guy as well.'

When Ryan Giggs was presented with his award, they had a Welsh male voice choir to perform in his honour. The funny thing was that when they finished he shook one of the singers' hands to say thank you and started to walk off. When you talk about father figures in football, I had Alan Buckley but Giggsy obviously had Fergie. The next minute, Fergie was calling over to him telling him to shake hands with the singers. Giggsy told him he had done but Fergie said, 'Not just that one – shake hands with the one next to him and the next one and the next one!'

There must have been about fifty of them but Fergie made Giggsy go back and shake all their hands. We thought Buckley was bad but Fergie really must have been like Giggsy's dad – he did exactly what he was told!

We got very well looked after that night and it showed that no matter how high up the echelons of football you go, there are still some very decent people. Ryan Giggs was a superstar that night. He has had some negative publicity more recently in his career but he deserves every accolade as far as I'm concerned.

Quite a lot of the players at the awards ceremony had games coming up so it was an early night for them and they were on the orange juice. But when it came to the after-show party, I was determined to make the most of the free bar – and I certainly took the right circle of friends to make the most of it. We were ordering round after round of Stellas – pretty soon every available space seemed to be covered in empty green bottles.

We had a fantastic night and I had my photograph taken with all kinds of people, like Fabio Capello, who was the England manager. We were probably the last ones out of the bar but even then when we got back to the hotel room, Lee had brought a bottle of champagne so we had a great end to the evening having a couple of glasses of bubbly each to round off the whole thing.

When we left, I noticed Lee had a long metal silver thing tucked under his arms. I asked him what on earth it was and he handed it over and said it was for me. It was the giant six-foot picture of me which the PFA had had on display on a stand at the awards. Lee had apparently asked someone if he could have it as a souvenir and when the guy started to say he wasn't sure if he was allowed to let him have it, Lee just whipped it away before he could stop him and was off down the corridor. Some people call it a life-size picture but it's over six feet and that's taller than I have ever been in my life!

I was told during the evening that it was a player called Scott McGleish who first got my name put forward for the award. I was chatting to him and Chris Powell, both of whom had been involved a lot in the PFA and it seemed that Ryan Giggs looked like being in contention to win both the Merit Award and the main Player of the Year award at one point. They were having meetings to discuss the awards and Scott told me he had suggested I should win the Merit Award instead of Giggsy.

He told them, 'I know this guy called John McDermott who played for the same team for twenty-odd years and people forget smaller clubs like Grimsby. These awards shouldn't be all about the high-profile names. He should get it.'

I am very grateful to him for that because he seemingly persuaded the rest of the PFA that I was someone who deserved the award and it's one of the biggest achieve-ments of my career.

Since winning the award I have been in touch several times with Gordon Taylor who has always been incredibly helpful to me. I contacted him once when a friend of mine was desperate for a ticket to an England game at Wembley because all his mates were going and he had somehow missed out. I rang Gordon and told him a bit of white lie – I said it was my brother-in-law but it was actually my next-door neighbour Chris Simpkins – sorry, Gordon!

I wasn't after a freebie, I was happy to pay for a ticket but he said there just weren't any left. However, he promised to see what he could do and arranged to meet my neighbour in a pub opposite the stadium. Chris went down there and was amazed to find Gordon Taylor there waiting for him exactly as arranged. And Gordon hadn't just got him a normal ticket – he had got him into one of the executive suites where all the VIPs are.

I was watching the game on the telly at home when my phone went and I got call from Chris,

> You won't believe where I am! They've all got expensive suits on and I'm here in my jeans. Lots of people are coming up to me and telling me they know you and what a great bloke you are. The only thing is they're asking questions about how many games you played and I've no idea.

Chris was in the toilets and I had to give him a quick run-down of my career so he didn't get found out as not being my brother-in-law after all. He was buzzing when he rang his mates in the normal seats on the other side of the ground, told them where he was and then waved to them to prove it.

The PFA sometimes gets a bad name because people tend to think of footballers at the top of the end of the game who earn a fortune and wonder why they need a union. I have got a lot of respect for Gordon Taylor because he is interested in grass roots football. The PFA isn't just a union that gives out awards, it is mostly about helping people with problems and helping players to sort out their future. There are players I know who have hit hard times after retiring and they have been able to tap into the PFA Benevolent Fund to get financial help. I can't speak highly enough of them.

# 21

# Learning Curve

After Lennie Lawrence was sacked in 2001, he told me that if I ever wanted to get my coaching badges done, I should get in touch. About a decade later it was through Lennie that I got my A Licence on one of the courses run by the Welsh FA. You need to get special dispensation to be enrolled on one of the Welsh FA courses if you're not actually Welsh and it was Lennie who got me on it.

There was a time when it was seen as being a slightly easier option to do the Welsh or Northern Irish course rather than the English one but in fact the Welsh course now has the reputation of being one of the best and lots of other countries have revamped theirs to bring them into line with what the Welsh FA do. It was a great course which I thoroughly enjoyed.

It was very intensive and right the way through I kept learning new things which made me think, 'That was something Lennie did' or 'Lennie used to do exactly that'. It made me realise that Lennie was ahead of his time by about ten years.

Those two weeks I spent in Cardiff were among the best times of my professional life and I made a lot of good friends from it. You get to a certain age and you think you know everything there is to know about football but these guys are absolutely top notch. The guy in charge of the course was the technical director Osian Roberts, who had been part of Gary Speed's coaching team and has also worked closely with Chris Coleman. His knowledge of the game is second to none and he was helped by a guy called Matt Bishop who went on to be Dean Holdsworth's assistant manager at Aldershot.

All the guys running that course were different class. I was blown away by it all. By the end, I felt I had learnt so much from it that even if I didn't pass it, it would have been well worth it.

I have been heartily recommending it ever since. It wasn't just the actual course content itself but just chatting to these guys about football in a relaxed atmosphere was really enjoyable. Osian is a big lad – in fact, you might think he was a rugby player rather than a footballer – but it was great to talk to him over a pint. His point was that you never get to the stage where you can't learn something new about football. Ian Rush came over to do a session for us and we also had a visit from Paul Jewell who I knew from my play-ing days. It is invaluable to hear first-hand the experiences of other managers and see things from their perspective.

To be a coach or a manager these days, you need to learn about plenty of things other than just football itself – there are related things like how you handle the media and how you handle players. These days you have to be media-savvy and you also have to be a psychologist. There were also ses-sions on the latest approaches to fitness on that course in Cardiff – I just took on board so much from it, I soaked it up like a sponge. Almost as soon as it was over, I was looking forward to going back for my refresher course.

As I have said before, you sometimes get given a helping hand at a club like Grimsby to start you off in management and maybe under different circumstances I might have been offered the assistant's job at Blundell Park and might never have bothered doing my coaching badges – because there was a time not so long ago when it was easy to get into management without the qualifications. I have had to go the other way and forge a career in coaching under my own steam although in many ways that has been good for my development. And nowadays if you haven't got the A Licence on your CV there's almost no point going to be interviewed for a manager's job.

It was when I was doing my UEFA A Licence in Wales that I was first sounded out about the Harrogate Town assistant manager's job. Matt Bloomer, who I had known from Grimsby Town, is a friend of the Harrogate manager Simon Weaver and put in a word for me when he heard that Simon was looking for an assistant. Simon rang me and explained what he was looking for; someone with tactical knowledge, setting teams up for set pieces, that kind of thing, and someone who would be able to go out and look at potential new players. I knew Simon anyway from my playing days because he had been at Lincoln City and one or two other clubs.

As I walked into Harrogate's ground for the interview in 2010, it was deja vu from when I arrived at Grimsby Town for the very first time. It was exactly the same feeling; a lovely sunny day, I bumped into the groundsman and had a chat with him about what a good state the pitch was in. I loved the ground and the atmosphere of the place and immediately felt at home there. When I met the chairman Bill Fotherby, he was a really memorable character who made quite an impression. He was nearly 80 years old but he looked like some kind of TV game show host with massive glasses on. Despite his age, he might as well have been 21 because he was as sharp as a tack.

Pretty soon I was in awe of him. There were lots of pictures of him on the walls mainly from his time at Leeds United, photos of him with all kinds of great names from recent football history. It was pretty clear I wasn't going to get one over him and he gave me a thorough interview.

Matty Bloomer had told me to mention during the interview an ex-player called Lee Philpott who was now an agent because he was someone that Bill particularly liked. So when Bill asked me if I knew many agents, I used the opportunity to drop Lee Philpott's name into the conversation and started to say what good friends we were. But Bill's face immediately went crimson.

'You know him, do you?' he started to say. But Weaves helped me out by butting in and saying, 'No, you don't really know him that well at all, do you, Macca?' because he knew that Philpott was no longer flavour of the month as he and Bill had had something of a fall-out over a player. Thanks, Blooms! He pretty much got me the job but then also nearly got me sacked within the first few minutes of my interview!

Fortunately, things were smoothed over OK and I got the job. Weaves and I have become really good mates since I took over as his assistant. We both have similar ambitions in football even though we came from different traditions of playing in many ways. My upbringing was all about Alan Buckley's style of passing the ball whereas Simon had been schooled more in the blood and guts approach of Keith Alexander. But that contrast works well because we rub off on each other and both benefit from each other's ideas.

Weaves had something of a rocky start at Harrogate and they finished bottom of the Conference North in his first season. Luckily they got a reprieve from relegation when Northwich Victoria got demoted instead because of their financial problems and it was at this point that I was appointed as assistant manager.

My first year at Harrogate Town was a real learning curve for me because I didn't really know that much about non-league. All my football knowledge was Football League, I didn't have many contacts with other managers or players at that lower level – but Weaves seemed to know everyone.

We played some great stuff pre-season but as soon as the league games started properly I could immediately see that we were a bit short of what was needed to do well in the Conference North but the budget was tight to bring new players in. At one point it looked as though the club was going to have to accept that it might need to go down a division or two to progress.

Bill had pretty much had enough, which was a great shame because he was such a loveable guy. You could see why players wanted to go there – I would have played myself for a chairman like that, I thought he was amazing. He was so infectious, I could sit in a room with him and just listen to him talking because he was an inspiration – and so many other people felt the same way. Bill was always full of passion for football and full of stories but the great thing about him if you were working for him was that he never put pressure on you. He wanted to win every game, of course, but as long as the lads gave their all he didn't get too upset about losing.

Simon's father Irving took over from Bill Fotherby as chairman of Harrogate Town after Weaves had been in charge for a while which did make some fans wonder whether the manager's job was just some kind of rich kid's hobby given to him by his sugar daddy. But I can tell you, nothing could be further than the truth. Weaves works his socks off at the job, he is always thinking about football and my wife goes mental because he is never off the phone talking to me about players and about matches we need to go and see to check on other teams.

It immediately gave me for the first time a real insight into the life of a football manager – and it's just the same for assistant managers. I always thought assistant managers' jobs were for single blokes because you were never at home, you were always out and about coaching or scouting. And if you weren't single when you started, you soon would be because your missus would divorce you! I wasn't far wrong, I can tell you – you have to have a very understanding wife.

When Bill stepped down as chairman and Simon's dad got involved, you could immediately tell that he was a shrewd businessman. He wasn't going to allow any complacency to creep in after Bill's departure and sure enough we soon got together a terrific squad who should probably have finished in the top six in 2011/12 – and I believe would have done if it hadn't been for a horrendous run of injuries. We were about seventh at one point but we had about eight players injured with everything from cruciates to hamstrings and then several others suspended because of bookings and sendings off. In the end we only ended up avoiding relegation on the last day of the season,

There has been a lot of investment at the club recently. Three stands have been refurbished, there's a new club shop and we have spent a fortune on the pitch, getting it levelled out properly and sorting out the drainage. Harrogate Town certainly feels like a club that's going places – I believe we could emulate a club like Burton Albion and get into the Football League, there's certainly enough ambition behind the scenes.

The people running the club are trying to do things the right way. They are not just pumping money in willy-nilly, which always ends up catching up with you in the end – they are trying to make the club self-sufficient and part of that is by attracting bigger crowds because that generates more revenue. Once you get up into the Conference Premier then you're only one step away from League 2 which has had all kinds of big clubs in there in recent years like Bradford City.

In fact it's teams like Bradford City that Harrogate Town could actually start competing with because a lot of football fans from Harrogate and Tadcaster travel over to Bradford to support them but with a bit more success we might start to pinch a few back and get them coming to watch us instead.

It is fair to say that it didn't take long for me to buy into what Harrogate Town are trying to achieve. Even the pre-season build-up was impressive – we travelled to Northern Ireland to play Crusaders, who were in the Europa League and playing Liverpool after they had played us. I soon found that we weren't having to ring up players chasing them – instead they were coming to us. And it wasn't because they thought they'd get a big pay day at Harrogate, they genuinely seemed excited about what we were trying to do at the club. In fact, if a player were to ring me and immediately started asking about what money we were offering, I would make a rule of thumb that we wouldn't sign them because they were coming for the cash rather than the football.

In my third season at Harrogate, we had a brilliant FA Cup run that put us in the limelight. In the earlier qualifying rounds we beat West Auckland and Frickley, which set us up with a game against Hyde for a place in the first round proper. That is when non-league sides get the chance to play a team from League 1 or League 2.

Hyde had been champions of our league, Blue Square North, the previous season so we knew all about them. They had played some great football and I thought it would be a big ask to beat them. But we had them watched quite a bit and the feedback we got was that they weren't as strong as they had been the year before. We had a game plan and we had just beaten our league leaders Brackley 6–1 so we were pretty confident going into that game.

Phil Jevons, an ex-Grimsby player funnily enough, put Hyde ahead from the penalty spot early on but we had the lion's share of the play and Leon Osborne deservedly got an equaliser in the 88th minute. By the time we played them again in the replay at our place, we knew the winners would be away to Torquay United. It was a strange draw for Harrogate because the last time they had made it to the first round proper, they were also drawn away to Torquay – on that occasion they held them to a draw but lost on penalties in the replay.

The fourth qualifying round replay had to take place at Harrogate Railway's ground because our pitch was unplayable after a lot of poor weather. Hyde played better in the second game but we nicked it 1–0 thanks to a Dan Clayton goal towards the end of extra time.

Although we had got through, lots of people seemed to be writing us off against Torquay. The replay had to be postponed twice because of the weather and didn't get it played in the end until the Wednesday before the first round proper tie at Plainmoor on the Saturday. Everyone seemed to think we had no chance because we would be exhausted and we would only have two days to get ready before travelling down to Devon. But we treated the whole thing very professionally; as soon as the draw was made we had started our preparations for Torquay on the assumption that we would beat Hyde. We had Torquay watched and I spoke to a couple of contacts who knew their team so we got a full rundown on all their players – we really did our homework.

I don't think Torquay had prepared properly for us. It certainly seemed to have thrown a spanner in the works having our replay against Hyde re-arranged twice even though their manager Martin Ling claimed they still knew enough about us to win. There was some talk from Torquay that there would be no need for a replay this time – and that was music to our ears.

Our lads were so up for the game, they were almost ripping the doors off their hinges to get out on to the pitch. Coming out of the tunnel at Plainmoor, it reminded me of the intensity we had at Grimsby when we played Northampton in the play-off final. I have never seen our lads like that, it was like they were going into a boxing match and the feeling I had was the same as I had at Wembley for that Northampton game. The manager and I glanced at each other as if to say, 'We're going to win this.'

I think Torquay maybe thought that because we were non-league we would be a team of overweight ex-players who were past their best and wouldn't be in great nick physically. They thought they would have the edge on us in terms of fitness – but what they didn't realise was that although our lads are only part-time at Harrogate, they go to the gym or go running in their own time five days a week and they're all in good shape. They are not all scaffolders like the traditional image of a non-league footballer. A lot of them are quite young lads who are in sports coaching and have come from professional football.

Our team that day had some really good young players like Tom Platt, a midfielder on loan from York City, and lads like Chib Chilaka and Luke Dean, who had both been at Bradford City, and the goalkeeper Craig MacGillivray. But we also had a lot of experience with people like Alan White, who was someone who kept himself fit like me even though he was in his mid-30s.

Things are very professional at Harrogate even though it's non-league. For example, the way the trip down to Torquay was organised was fantastic. We stayed overnight and were quite keen to do some training as soon as we arrived at the hotel but it was dark because the coach journey had taken so long. The hotel had indoor tennis courts where we thought we could at least have a session to get rid of some of the stiffness from being on the road. But they weren't modern courts, they were Victorian, with old-fashioned wooden floors.

It was an amazing place where you had to feed a meter to get the lights going. After a while the lights went out and it was absolutely pitch black, you couldn't see a thing. We were stumbling around for ages waiting for someone to get more money and when the lights finally did come back on – there were two of our lads stripped stark naked. One had the other one bent over the tennis net and they were pretending they had just been caught in the act. They picked up their neat piles of clothes and trotted off sheepishly saying, 'Sorry!'

We were falling about laughing. How they managed to pull off a joke like that so quickly and get their clothes off in the dark, I'll never know. Things like that really showed how relaxed everyone was even though they had a massive FA Cup game the next day. It gave me a feeling that the team had a real togetherness and that something special was going to happen against Torquay.

Martin Ling had said before the game that Torquay would have to play poorly and Harrogate would have to play above ourselves for us to win. Well, he was half right because his team were poor that day but what he didn't realise was that we didn't have to raise our game – how we played that day was the level we had already been playing at for several weeks.

Torquay are a good side and had been doing well in League 2 but some of our football that afternoon was breathtaking. It wasn't a shock when we got the goal through Chib Chilaka because we were playing so well but even so we celebrated like crazy. Torquay had some chances to equalise, don't get me wrong, but if you look at the stats, their keeper actually made more saves than ours so we felt we were worthy winners. It was a great feeling when the final whistle blew because we had made history – it was the first time Harrogate had ever made it through to the second round proper of the FA Cup.

It was a magical feeling and you could tell how much it meant to everyone. Players were rushing up to staff and giving them big hugs – it was really quite moving.

For the sheer sense of what had been achieved, that win over Torquay was on a par with Wembley for me. They were different emotions in a way because as a player you can only control your own performance so there is a sense of self-achievement. It is different as a coach or manager because you have less control over what happens on the pitch but you get a great sense of satisfaction from feeling that you have helped put together a team that's achieved something special. That was my best day in management – so far!

We pulled Hastings out of the hat for the next round, which wasn't the glamour tie we had been hoping for but it gave us a good chance of getting through to the third round proper when the Premier League and Championship clubs enter the competition. When our game at home to

Hastings finished 1–1, we found out that the winners of the replay would play Middlesbrough away in the next round – what a draw for me!

Sadly, we lost the replay on penalties after Tom Platt had scored a last-minute equaliser to take it to extra time. There was a real buzz around the club thanks to that FA Cup run, both those games against Hastings were on TV and we had Sky cameras around the ground for several days. It seemed like Weaves was never off the telly! All credit to him because the management team have worked really hard for three years now and deserve their success.

Looking back at when I was interviewed for the Grimsby Town manager's position in 2009, I was obviously disappointed not to get it because I went into it quite confidently. I knew what I wanted to bring to the job and I had prepared well, much better than when I was interviewed by Boston United. But it would have been my first job in management and I would have been something of a novice.

All the experience I have since gained at Harrogate has been invaluable and I know it would make me a much better manager now. In the past, when it came to tweaking the team I would have probably ended up relying on what I had available and might have tried to put square pegs in round holes. Now I feel I have learnt so much more and have built up some great contacts so I would be able to look at my team and properly work out which areas needed changing and what sort of new players I would want to bring in.

In hindsight, with Grimsby Town being so close to my heart, maybe it was for the best that I didn't get the manager's job back in 2009. Who knows in the future? If that job comes up again, I'm going to be in a much better position to do it justice, that's for sure. Maybe that will be another chapter in my story.

# Macca's Choice

And finally...

I couldn't finish without picking out some of the best players I've played with and against during my career.

## My Best Grimsby Town XI

Paul Crichton (Goalkeeper)
 Excellent hands, a great shot stopper and could pick a player out anywhere on the pitch with either foot.

Bobby Cummings (Right-back)
 When he played there he was as hard as nails, fit as a butcher's dog and took no prisoners – a true pro.

Peter Handyside (Centre-back)
 He was our Alan Hansen – but drank more. A quality passer.

Andy Todd (Centre-back)
 Best defender I have played alongside, he read the game so well. Andy was hard but fair and wouldn't just kick

it away but always played his way out of trouble. Pure class.

## Gary Croft (Left-back)

This was a hard position to choose between Gary Croft and Tony Gallimore. Crofty was more like me and liked to bomb on. He also went on to bigger things so I will go with Crofty. Gally – you're sub, mate.

## Gary Childs (Right-wing)

I played with some great wide players like Tommy Watson, Kev Donovan and Gary Childs but because I went through the leagues with Childsy I'm going for Gaz.

## Dave Gilbert (Left-wing)

Without doubt the best player with the ball in my time at Grimsby. 'Diddy' ever lose it? Very rarely! And he had the biggest calves in the game – after mine.

## Wayne Burnett (Centre midfield)

Tricky, very clever on the ball and brave – not necessarily in the tackle but wanted the ball all the time.

## Jim Dobbin (Centre midfield)

Very similar to Wayne but probably a better passer. Sorry Waz!

## Tony Rees (Striker)

Legs like Mark Hughes but bigger. You could knock the ball into him anywhere on the field and he would get hold of it and link the play up. Loved a backheel.

Clive Mendonca (Striker)
Super Clive Mendonca – a goal machine. He led the line no problem and would get you a goal from nothing. You always had a chance of winning a game with Clive in your team.

**Subs:**

Mark Lever – solid, no frills, a great lad who knew his job and did it well.

Tony Gallimore – pushes Crofty close for a place in the starting XI.

Paul Groves – true pro who scored goals. A big-game player and a great leader.

Phil Bonnyman – as a kid I watched him and managed to play alongside him for a while. He oozed class.

Neil Woods – a mixture between Rees and Mendonca.

Nigel Batch – so close to 'Crotch' for the goalkeeper's spot but I only played with him in thirteen games. Both of them were similar keepers and both were pure class.

Kev Donovan – great understanding, telepathic at times. He was a pleasure to play alongside, tore defences to bits and also scored goals.

Steve Livingstone – great touch for a big lad, ran his socks off and could get you a goal. Livvo was also a nutter!

# The Best Opponents I Have Come Up Against In My Career

And here is Macca's Super Seven:

1. Alan Comfort (Leyton Orient and Middlesbrough)
A very tricky winger who was similar to our own Dave Gilbert, good with both feet, he could chop and change. Sadly Alan had to retire early because of injury and is now a vicar who is club chaplain at Leyton Orient.

2. Darren Eadie (Norwich City and Leicester City)
Darren was especially difficult to play against for Norwich because they were very strong down the left of their team. They also had Robert Ullathorne on that side and Keith O'Neill up front. It was always a battle against Darren. You always knew you had been in a game with him and nine times out of ten my hamstrings would have gone by the end of 90 minutes.

3. Ted McMinn (Derby County)
They used to call him the Tin Man. He reminded me of Steve McManaman because he was very tricky but he was old school and a bit of a character. Ted loved to have a laugh and a joke with the crowd and liked to talk to the defenders who were marking him so they wouldn't kick him. Sadly he got an infection in his foot after he retired and had to have it amputated.

4. Tommy Wright (Leicester City)
Similar to Alan Comfort, he never gave you an easy ride. Tommy never seemed to get tired because he was as fit as a butcher's dog. It was always a pleasure playing against him.

5. Peter Beagrie (Sheffield United and Bradford City)
Peter had lots of tricks up his sleeve and loved to do drag-backs. He was another one who could chop and change direction which made it difficult to play against. It was tough being up against him at Sheffield United when he had Peter Withe in the middle banging in all his crosses. Beags was also a good pro who looked after himself and played a lot of games.

6. Steve McManaman (Liverpool)
Steve was the quickest player I have ever come across. He could certainly run faster with the ball than anyone I have known. He loved a bit of banter with the crowd and when I played him I would be cramping up but he would be having a chat with me during the game and would then suddenly say, 'Got to go and join in again now.' Steve really was quality.

7. Lee Philpott (Cambridge United and Leicester City)
I played against Lee right the way up through the leagues from the old Fourth Division when he was at Cambridge. I didn't mind playing against Lee but you knew it was always going to be a tough game. You didn't know whether to bomb on against him because Cambridge were quite direct and you were worried about getting caught out by his pace.

# Index